Prayer Seeds

A Gathering of Blessings,

Reflections, and Poems

for Spiritual Growth

JOYCE RUPP

SORIN BOOKS NOTRE DAME, IN

Scripture quotations are from *New Revised Standard Version Bible*, copyright © 1989 National Council of the Churches of Christ in the United States of America. Used by permission. All rights reserved.

Lyrics from "Darkness Cover Me," are reprinted with permission of Sara Thomsen. All rights reserved.

"Great Traveler" is reprinted from *Prayer*, ©2007 by Joyce Rupp. Used by permission of Orbis Books.

"When Someone Deeply Listens to You," from *Finding What You Didn't Lose*, by John Fox, copyright © 1995 by John Fox. Used by permission of Tarcher, an imprint of Penguin Publishing Group, a division of Penguin Random House LLC.

"The Second Coming," by Jessica Powers, from *The Selected Poetry of Jessica Powers*, published by ICS Publications, Washington, DC. All copyrights, Carmelite Monastery, Pewaukee, WI. Used with permission.

www.sorinbooks.com

Paperback: ISBN-13 978-1-933495-98-9

E-book: ISBN-13 978-1-933495-99-6

Cover image © iStockphoto.com.

Cover design by Brian C. Conley.

Text design by K. H. Bonelli.

Printed and bound in the United States of America.

Library of Congress Cataloging-in-Publication Data is available.

CONTENTS

INTRODUCTION

~⌒⌐

To plant a seed
is to activate the deepest mysteries
of the Universe.
—Thomas Berry

*S*eeds have fascinated me ever since my youth when I lived on a farm
in northwest Iowa. Each year I observed my mother planting her large
garden with vegetable and flower seeds while my father sowed the fields
of black earth with kernels of corn, soybeans, and oats. Over the summer I
enjoyed watching all this come to life, amazed at the greening and growth
emerging from the plantings. When autumn arrived, happiness skipped inside
of me as we gathered the garden's abundance and loaded the heaping wagons
with golden grain from the fields. All of this coming from what was once small,
nondescript seeds.

What a truly wondrous process—so much life within a seed when it is
cared for and tended. Each resource in this book is a type of spiritual seed. The
selections hold the possibility of yielding a harvest of personal reflection and
communal prayer. Some are in the germination stage and will require watering
from additional ideas and resources in order to fully activate the potential they
hold. Others are partially grown and will only need minor tending. A handful
of selections in *Prayer Seeds* are fully grown and ready for use, supplying all
that is needed for harvesting a prayerful experience.

As with *Out of the Ordinary* (my previous book containing blessings,
reflections and poems), some of these prayer seeds were first planted when I
created them for retreats, conferences, and workshops. This time, however, a
number of the current resources were developed when it was my turn to lead
our small group of ten women who gather for prayer every Tuesday morning.
We call ourselves the "Morning Midwives" because of our intent to support
the ongoing birth of spiritual growth in one another. We come from diverse
religious backgrounds and professions. During the eight years we have been
together a profound spiritual kinship has evolved. I believe a good portion of
this is a result of how we choose to begin each gathering by deliberately greeting
one another in a reverential way.

Namasté

You will note that a number of the prayer seeds in this book begin with *Namasté*. This salutation comes from the practice of people in India and other Eastern cultures who use this to greet one another accompanied by a gentle bow (instead of our "hello" or "hi"). *Namasté* in the Western world often lacks some of the fullness of its original intent. Various Western interpretations allude to it as "I greet the Holy One in you." A woman who resided in India for five years explained, "To greet another with *Namasté* is to say, I greet the totality of who you are, your deepest self where your true being resides and I greet the part of you with its flaws and incompleteness that is still in the process of becoming whole."

This explanation expanded my understanding and led me to a fuller approach in using the greeting. From my Christian tradition I now perceive *Namasté* to acknowledge the fullness of divinity or goodness at the core of one's being, along with an acceptance of the unfinished part of self that continues in the ongoing process of transformation. *Namasté* welcomes another as the Beloved and accepts each one's less-than-perfect-self with compassionate non-judgment.

Thus, when each of us "Morning Midwives" stands in a circle and extends this greeting at the beginning of our morning prayer it is as if we are saying, "Here we are, with divinity shining in us. Here we are, beauty-full, and still having considerable development yet to happen before that Light shines in fullness. I accept you as you are and cheer you on to the growth that awaits you." Through this initial opening of prayer, the reverence we have for one another deepens and expands by our acknowledgment of each one's inner gold.

Here is how we proceed with the greeting. The person to the left of the facilitator of prayer and reflection for that day begins by speaking her name. We all respond with a gentle bow to her, repeating the name and then greeting a quality of goodness in her (one chosen by the facilitator). We continue going around the standing circle until all have been greeted.

For example, on a day when the topic of prayer was Enduring Love, the person to the left of the facilitator spoke her name: "Kathy." All bowed toward Kathy and responded, "*Namasté*, Kathy. I greet the Enduring Love in you." The next person spoke her name, "Mary." All responded, bowing, "*Namasté*, Mary. I greet the Enduring Love in you." We continued in this manner with the remaining women who were present.

The qualities of goodness with which we have addressed each other after our *Namasté* have been vast. Some of these include

> I greet the Compassionate One in you.
> I greet the kindness in you.
> I greet the spirit of the ancestors in you.
> I greet the strength to endure in you.
> I greet the gift of laughter in you.
> I greet the dancing muse of creativity in you.
> I greet the listening heart in you.
> I greet the radiant light in you.
> I greet the deep peace in you.
> I greet the gift of hope in you.
> I greet the Holy One's strength in you.
> I greet the divine beauty in you.
> I greet the playful child in you.
> I greet the strength to surrender in you.
> I greet the Beloved One in you.

To refresh our intention of *Namasté*, one morning we spoke the following to each one: "*Namasté*, _____. You are a temple of Love." We then paused for ten seconds to deepen this reality, focusing on the woman we greeted. The facilitator then rang a small bell and the next person gave her name and we greeted her with "*Namasté*, _____. You are a temple of Love," continuing with the pause and bell ringing until all had been welcomed as a "temple of Love."

For added emphasis on the deep connection shared among us, we occasionally greet one another with mutuality, such as: "The Compassionate One in me honors the Compassionate One in you." On another occasion, after each one announced her name we rekindled our reverence by bowing silently, not using any words at all. In another instance, the week after Joyce, one of our treasured members, died, the facilitator invited us to welcome each other with, "*Namasté*, _____. I greet the spirit of Joyce that lives on in you."

This manner of greeting one another with respect, non-judgment, and gratitude holds endless possibilities. It is my hope that groups gathering for a spiritual practice might begin their prayer times in a similar mode. What a difference in tone and attitude this can make for those who intend to pray together.

Using This Book

Many of the prayers and blessings in this book are designed to be used in communal settings. The role of the leader is often specified. Although other roles are not specified, you are encouraged to assign roles such as "reader" to members of the group.

The sources of the various quotes and readings found in this collection are listed in the References section. In some of the prayers you will find suggestions for appropriate songs. Lyrics and recordings of the songs can be easily found using the Internet.

Permission to Use Published Material with Acknowledgment

Ave Maria Press, Inc., has graciously honored my request that the resources contained in this book may be copied for personal and liturgical use without requiring permission from the publishing company. It is imperative, however, that you give adequate acknowledgement to the source of the piece you are copying. Much published work is lost because of carelessness or hurriedness when the source is not included on a printed page. Copying published work without including the title, author and publishing company is like visiting the home of a friend and deciding to borrow something valued from that friend's household and then never returning it. Please take the time and have the kindness to acknowledge the source when you print something from this book.

Each page you reproduce must include the following credit line: Taken from *Prayer Seeds: A Gathering of Blessings, Reflections, and Poems for Spiritual Growth* © 2017 by Joyce Rupp. Used by permission of Ave Maria Press, Inc. All rights reserved.

Gratitude

Thank you, each reader and user of the material in *Prayer Seeds*. What joy I have in believing that you desire to be a person who not only prays but can be enriched in being a person of prayer by using these resources. I hope that your experience draws you ever closer to the heart of the Holy One.

Advent

and

Christmas

A CHRISTMAS PRAYER

Emmanuel, God-with-us,
you chose to come for each person,
the destitute and the wealthy,
the unfortunate and the privileged,
the troubled and the peaceful,
the healthy and the ill.

You came in human form
with a message of extravagant love,
showing us how to be with those
who have much less than we do.
You came offering a gesture
of respect and reverence
instead of indifference and disdain;
giving courteous kindness
in place of thoughtless disregard;
contributing ongoing support
rather than a mere holiday handout.

Change my heart.
Turn it inside out,
toward the larger world.
Remind me daily of those who struggle
with their basic existence.
Lead me to help change social systems
that contribute to this ongoing struggle.
Enlarge my awareness.
Increase my generosity.
Guide my choices of how I live,
what I purchase,
and how I use my material wealth.

Remind me often of your presence
in those I tend to ignore or forget.

Boundless Love,
thank you for cherishing each person
on this planet.

BE STILL

~

Be still, and know that I am God.

—Psalm 46:10

The silence is there within us.
We have to enter it to become silent,
to become the silence.

—John Main

On the table: a circle of small lit candles with a larger lit candle in the center of them. Small papers with the words "Be Still" are scattered between the candles.

Introduction

Leader: In these days before Christmas, there are many things that can keep us from the stillness ready to open us to the wonder and beauty of Emmanuel. Physical illness, emotional and mental distress, social commitments, deadlines at work, relationship differences, shopping, correspondence, and other stressful situations can disquiet us. Let us pause to regain stillness so we can enter these Advent days with a peaceful spirit as we prepare for the great feast of Christmas.

Greeting

Stand in silence and greet the Sacred Stillness in one another. The person being greeted folds his/her hands over the heart. All gaze on this person for a moment and then bow quietly. The next one then folds hands over the heart and all greet that person with a bow. Continue until all have been greeted.

Song

"Be Still," *Seven Sacred Pauses*, Velma Frye, or
"Be Still," *O Healing Light of Christ*, Carey Landry, or
"Be Still," *Unfolding*, Trish and Richard Bruxvoort-Colligan.

Reading 1: from *The Grace in Aging*, Kathleen Dowling Singh

We need to create havens of quiet.

Interior silence allows us to be receptive to insight and to remain mindful of intention. It empties the mind and, in that emptying, allows us the experience of grace.

Reading 2: from *Living with Christ*, Patricia Livingston

God is love and whoever remains in love remains in God and God in [them] (1 John 4:16). This verse is one of the best doorways for me into the mystery that is God. . . . I once read that the Greek word translated here as "remain in" can also be translated as "settle in for a while and relax." In challenging times, I am grateful to be reminded to ponder all the ways that love is in my life and feel myself relax, knowing that I am settling into the arms of God.

Pause for an extended time of quiet meditation, to dwell in stillness

Leader: Breathe deeply and slowly, opening your mind.
Inhale and exhale, setting aside your long list of things to do.
Breathe deeply and slowly, opening your heart.
Inhale and exhale, letting peace reveal itself within you.
Breathe deeply and slowly, opening your whole being.
Inhale and exhale, letting your peace go forth to the world.

Song

See options above.

Intercessions

Response: **May they find Christ in the stillness of their hearts.**
Leader: Let us call to mind those whose lives are filled with continual activity
Parents with small children . . .
Over-worked church staffs . . .
Laborers in factories and small businesses . . .
Construction workers . . .

Store clerks . . .
Teachers . . .
Medical personnel . . .
Additional groups may be added.

Closing Prayer

L	*eader:* Silent One, as we move within our daily tasks, clothe us with your peace-filled stillness. With the cloak of your all-embracing quietness we can be assured of remaining focused on what you desire of us. May our external activities be such that they enable us to stay mindful of you. May our spirits be quiet enough to welcome you. Slow us down when we want to speed up. Move us toward that quiet pool of peace inside of us where we can be attentive to your love. In these days before Christmas, draw us ever nearer to you in all we are and do. Protect us from whatever drives peace away. Anchor us in your love. Amen.

CHRISTMAS BIRTHING

Christmas.

Memory of the Great Birthing,
the Holy One emerging
from the womb of Mary,

coming with a heart
wide enough
to embrace the one and the many
with the fullness of acceptance.

Christmas.
More than a memory.

Invitation:
embrace the one and the many
now
with the same wide love.

Open what is closed,
Widen what is narrow,
Make love large where it is small.

Keep birthing Christ into the world.

Let this wide love
emerge from the womb
of your Christmas-self.

CHRISTMAS THEN AND NOW

Then

Into the chasm of emptiness came the Fullness of Life.
Into the endless searching came the Attentive Listener.
Into the constant struggle came the Tireless Peace Giver.
Into the deep despair came the Heart of Hope.
Into the desolation came the Divine Consolation.
Into the woundedness came the Gentle Healer.
Into the void of joy came the Source of Happiness.
Into the bewilderment came the Spirit of Clarity.
Into the ache of heart came the Compassionate One.
Into the worried fretting came the Trustworthy Presence.
Into the search for meaning came the Wise Teacher.
Into the gulf of grief came the Loving Embrace.
Into the bleak darkness came the Light of the World.

Now

We are the ones birthing this Love into life.
We are the greeting of hospitality for the lonely.
We are the source of comfort for the sorrowing.
We are the rock of courage for the weakened.
We are the bearer of hope for the despondent.
We are the gift of acceptance for the rejected.
We are the voice of justice for the powerless.
We are the touch of healing for the wounded.
We are the sound of joy for the disheartened.
We are the home of welcome for the lost one.
We are the conveyer of trust for the self-doubter.
We are the calm dwelling for the anxiety-ridden.
We are the resting place for the worn and weary.

We are the Light of the World. Christ lives in us.

DISCOVER DIVINE PRESENCE

May we look for your goodness in others when it hides beneath layers of coldness.

May we behold your radiance in the ones we neglect or spurn at home or work.

May we discover your love in our deepest self when we feel unloving and irritable.

May we embrace you in the persons whose faithfulness we take for granted.

May we see your empathy in those serving the wounded of the world.

May we recognize your courage in the valiant people who speak out for justice.

May we notice your non-judgmental acceptance in those who keep an open mind.

May we search for your gentleness when the harshness of another hides it.

May we observe your generosity in every gift we receive, no matter how small the gift.

May we reveal your mercy when we pardon someone for having turned against us.

May we welcome your joy in the delightful voices and the easy play of children.

May we convey your compassion when we visit those with illness and poor health.

May we detect your patience in those who put up with our impatience and hurry.

May we unite with your peace hidden beneath the layers of humanity's disharmony.

Jesus, you came into our world in the form of a newly emerged child, fresh and fragile like all of us at our birthing. You came as a cherished one filled with the radiance of eternal Light. As you grew in humanness, your life and teachings revealed the vast goodness of your inner being. We now carry your loving Spirit of Radiance within us. We can neglect this gift in the press of our activities and clouded vision. Skim away the inattentiveness of our minds and the crusts of unloving on our hearts. As we prepare to celebrate the wonder of your birth, help us discern your concealed presence in each piece of our life. Amen.

DIVINE LOVE INCARNATE IN US

When divine love becomes incarnate in us, Christ is born anew.
—Ilia Delio

For several weeks I meditated on the photos in Margaret Woodson Nea's precious book, *Children, Eyes of the Soul.* Each page contains a photo of a child from a distant country. Their fresh eyes hold calm expectation and profound trust. These young ones are the epitome of soul seeing. Each child's photo expresses inner clarity, reminding me to shake loose the clutter from my heart, from my life, so love can reign supreme. They speak to me of Jesus who also came as a young one, who brought and kept his fresh soul's vision of how to create a world of loving kindness.

This Advent, make a personal commitment to look more intentionally and clearly, to engage in "soul seeing." Welcome the One Great Love more fully into your life and extend that Love to others. Here are some ways to do this:

> Look into the eyes of children. See a reflection of the hidden possibilities in your own being for uncluttered joy, clarity of outlook, and unconditional love.

> Look beneath the differences and disagreements separating you from others. See the One Great Love dwelling inside those you prefer to ignore or rebuff.

> Look beyond impatience and discouragement when tasks remain undone. See loving presence as more vital than achievement or the completing of goals.

> Look closely at those who gather for church and social events. See how each person carries burdens that can be eased by a gesture of welcome, a word of kindness.

> Look at the Christmas cards and variety of gifts received. See the attention and care that accompanied the sending and the giving.

> Look with eyes of wonder at the daily turning of night's darkness into daylight. See a similar pattern within yourself—the Christ-Light

turning the darkness of your unloving into expressions of light-filled care and kindheartedness.

Look at Christmas crèche scenes. See the story of Love, the birth of Jesus whose gift of presence and teachings continue to offer inspiration and hope.

*C*hild of Bethlehem, open the eyes of my heart. Reveal your love in these Advent days as I prepare to celebrate your birth into our world. Child of Peace, open the tightly closed shades of my mind. I want to dispel my skepticism and doubt regarding the possibility of world peace. Child of Wonder, uncover me from the blankets of busyness that lay heavily upon my days. Lift my gaze to rest upon the beauty that is ready for me to behold in the most simple and the most elegant of faces and places. May I look with the free gaze of a child newly born. Let me see as you see. Amen.

Epiphany Blessing

The story of the astrologers who traveled to the Christ Child by following a star has endless implications for those of us who live in this present age. For we, too, are seekers. We, too, travel by faith, not knowing how long or how far we must go before we encounter Christ, the One Love of our hearts. Like the Wise Ones, we see the Star, lose sight of the Star, find the Star again. Like them, we do not give up our desire to discover the One Love who waits to guide our way.

May you listen to your soul-stirrings urging you to leave the home of your satisfactions, to risk new discoveries by traveling into the "land of don't know."

May you allow yourself to be guided by the Star of Grace, with the assurance of an abiding faith, as you seek the path of spiritual growth.

May you be willing to journey with vulnerability in the land of darkness and obscurity when the way fills with uncertainty.

May you have the gift of discerning what draws you forward, and what leads you away, in seeking the One Love.

May you find inspiration, courage, and hope through your kinship with others who also journey by faith on the road of life.

May you have openness of mind and heart so that you recognize the divine Star in those whose demeanor conceals this light-filled love.

May you daily bring the gift of your truest self and offer this to the Revealer of Love, who knows the bounty of your virtues.

May you be filled with gratitude each time you discover the One Love in some aspect of your life.

May the joy that the Wise Travelers expressed upon discovering the Christ Child also dance within your heart.

MAKE ROOM FOR EMMANUEL

There was no place for them in the inn.
—Luke 2:7

This prayer may be used in a group or individually. In a group setting two leaders may alternately read the first part of each petition with the group responding: **Help me make room for you in my heart, Emmanuel.**

When I become overly-engaged in life's activities and allow them to crowd out space for essential prayer and reflection, help me make room for you in my heart, Emmanuel.

When the pain of a world weary with war and violence threatens my hope and diminishes my belief in the goodness of humanity, help me make room for you in my heart, Emmanuel.

When I am asked to forgive another's failings or to let go of old hurts that cling stubbornly to my aggrieved self, help me make room for you in my heart, Emmanuel.

When I give undue attention to myself, or when excessive preoccupation with my own schedule tempts me to ignore the needs of others, help me make room for you in my heart, Emmanuel.

When jealousy or resentment of another's good fortune takes away from my gratitude for all I have been given, help me make room for you in my heart, Emmanuel.

When another's religion, skin color, sexual orientation, or personal beliefs differ from my own, help me make room for you in my heart, Emmanuel.

When the heartache and distress of those dear to me saddens my spirit and suffocates my desire to bring joy to others, help me make room for you in my heart, Emmanuel.

When peace seems far away from my deeper self, and crushing distress pays daily visits to my body, mind, or spirit, help me make room for you in my heart, Emmanuel.

>When the day is done and I look over the hours that have passed before I rest my head on the pillow of sleep, help me make room for you in my heart, Emmanuel.

When I join friends and family to celebrate the gift of your birth in human form and gather to remember your boundless love, help me make room for you in my heart, Emmanuel.

All: Emmanuel, God-with-us, you stand at the door of my heart and await my welcome. Help me be aware of your presence each day in the people who enter my life. I desire to open my heart, to make room for you in any part of self that tends to keep you out. Show me those places where you still need a welcome. Spur on my courage to open the door and invite you in. I want to make room for you in my heart, Emmanuel.

Restoring Awareness

Respond to each of the following intercessions: **Restore my awareness of your light-filled presence.**

Come, show us how you are dwelling in those places of our lives where we have forgotten to welcome you . . .

Come, take us to the place where you are moving us toward change and deeper relationship with you . . .

Come, help us believe in the possibility of resurrecting what has hidden itself from our path of growth . . .

Come, shake free whatever keeps us from accepting your invitation to be transformed . . .

Come, strengthen our faith, cultivate our hope, and widen our love . . .

Come, draw us into the stillness essential for an alive and open awareness of your presence . . .

Come, keep us mindful of the larger world, one in urgent need of our compassion and dedicated care . . .

Come, be a healing presence for those who suffer, and those for whom we have promised to pray . . .

Come, our minds and hearts are alert, ready to welcome you home . . .

All: Holy One, awaken my heart. Quiet my mind. Draw back the veil of my illusions to perceive your presence. Settle what stirs endlessly within me. Hush the voice of haste and hurry. Awaken my inner senses to recognize your love hiding beneath the frenzy. Enfold me in your attentiveness. Wrap a mantle of mindfulness around every part of my days. I want to welcome you with joy and focus on your dwelling place. Amen.

SILENT NIGHT, HOLY NIGHT

"Silent night, holy night,"
lyrics calling the soul to stillness,
singing of deeper wakefulness,
drawing the heart toward the One
whose presence bears inner peace.

What has happened to our stillness?

"Silent night, holy night,"
a meaningless white noise
filling the consumerized air,
words of forgotten worth
laid aside for the latest store sales,
lost in the dullness of endless rushing,
buried in turmoiled relationships.

Now is the time to return
to the stillness that elicits peace.
Now is the moment to revisit
the inner chambers of deafness
and reopen them to wonder.

O Christ of the Soul's Stillness,
quiet the clamoring din of impatience.
Slow the hurry of unrelenting steps.
Lessen the voices clamoring for attention.
Silence the useless anxiety and confusion.
Calm the pressures placed upon us.
Hush the illusory need *to get it all done*.

Come and soothe our weariness.
Settle whatever disturbs our serenity.
Bring us home to you again and again,
to the steady stillness abiding in our depths.
Then we can welcome your presence
however and wherever your love is birthed.

All Saints,
All Souls

A Blessing of the Saints

~

This reflection is best used when one person slowly leads an individual or a group through the visualization. Invite those entering into the meditation to find a comfortable place and peaceful bodily position for the meditation.

Begin by relaxing and quieting your body, mind, and spirit.
Pay attention to your breath; notice how the breath comes in and moves out.
Let yourself feel contentment, joy, peace.
Allow a sense of deep trust to fill you.

Go within to a deeper part of your being.
Picture yourself in a place that is safe, sacred, quiet.
Make yourself comfortable in this place.
See the outlines of white-robed figures in the distance.
They are moving toward you with an easy flow of goodness and grace.
You can sense the energy of their love and belief in you.

Each of those coming has been a source of blessing.
The white-robed figures proceed toward you, one by one.
As they move, they gaze at you with fondness and hope.

One of these beings who nurtured your body or your spirit approaches.
This life-giver comes close and blesses you.

Next, a mentor or teacher who imparted wisdom arrives.
This wise one draws near and also blesses you.

Now someone who urged you to take risks appears by your side.
Let this encouraging and challenging one extend a blessing.

Then all approach who helped you to become the person you are today.
These beloved ones form a circle around you and offer their blessing.
Look at these many white-robed beings extending love.
Thank them for what they have done, and then bid these special ones farewell.

With these blessings in your heart, visualize yourself standing up with your arms outstretched toward the universe. See yourself moving slowly in a circle, facing all four directions as you turn. Love goes forth from you to all of creation. Let yourself be a blessing for the world.

Now, slowly return to this time and place. Take some time to respond to the meditation. *This could be through music, prayer, drawing, painting, journaling, or some other way of your choice.*

All Souls Day

The response is: **We entrust them to your abiding love.** *Pause briefly to remember after each of the following is named.*

> Those taken from us all too soon . . .
> All who died while incarcerated . . .
> People afflicted with a terminal disease . . .
> Children stillborn or miscarried . . .
> First responders who died trying to save lives . . .
> Persons who took their own lives . . .
> Those who suffered from addictions . . .
> Missionaries, pastors, and staff members . . .
> Loved ones who slipped away without warning . . .
> Fearful ones who did not die peacefully . . .
> Victims of war, violence, and abuse of any form . . .
> Persons surprised by death during surgery . . .
> Elderly men and women and those in nursing homes . . .
> People who left without extending forgiveness . . .
> Men and women who died while at work . . .
> Traffic accident fatalities and homicide victims . . .
> Parents who left behind their young children . . .
> Those filled with excruciating, unbearable pain . . .
> Persons who lived unknown and lonely lives . . .
> Each person dear to our hearts whom we miss today . . .

Prayer together: We turn to you, Comforter and Sustainer of Hope. We remember the presence of those we knew. Once more we entrust them to your abiding love, praying for their peace and ours, too. We gather strength from kinship with those whose hearts also ache with the absence of their loved ones. Grant us freedom from our grief. With your grace we will surrender as best we can to the mystery of death and what lies beyond it. In you we place our trust. Amen.

Strength of the Ancestors

~

They are in us, those long departed ones.
They are in our inclinations, our moral burdens, our pulsing blood,
and in the gestures that arise from the depths of time.
—Rainer Maria Rilke

Introduction

Leader: Many religious and indigenous communities honor the ancestors who shaped and formed their beliefs and rituals. Christians honor their central ancestor, Jesus, and also remember those whose lives were shaped by his teachings. We do so each time we celebrate Eucharist, with the naming of individuals in the Eucharistic Prayer. In particular, on the feast of All Saints, we pay homage to the saints, whether canonized or not. In doing so, we are meant to be renewed and reinspired in our journey of spiritual transformation. We do not limit this feast only to those officially recognized for their holiness by the Church. Numerous women and men who have gone before us are sources of encouragement by the way they lived as persons of strong faith and great love. Let us today recall the strength of these persons and give thanks.

Prayer

Namasté. I greet the strength of the ancestors in you.
Leader: In the spirit of indigenous people who believe in their unity with the ancestors, and who often call these spirits forth into their gatherings, let us call forth into our midst the presence, the memory, and the strength of those who influenced and shaped our beliefs and values.

Prayer (alternate sides): Spirit of our ancestors,
this day we join in acknowledging the blessedness
of the many who inspired us and shaped our faith.

We turn in memory and appreciation
toward those ancestors in our family of origin
who influenced and encouraged us to live as our best selves.

We remember, too, those ancestors who left this world
with hurts unresolved. We open our deep self to you
and pray that any woundedness we've inherited
will be healed through your grace and our love-filled hearts.

We bring to mind others beyond family who enriched our lives
and led us further on our journey of personal transformation.
We honor all those who sacrificed and suffered
in order for peace and justice to be furthered on our planet.

We give thanks and rejoice for the countless, unnamed persons
whose lives left a lasting mark of kindness and compassion.

May the remembrance of each of these blessed ones
inspire and increase our personal commitment
to leave a trace of goodness wherever we go.

When we depart this sphere of life may our inner strength
have contributed to individual and world peace.

Reading: from *Abbey of the Arts*, Newsletter, Christine Valters Paintner

The Christian feasts of All Saints and All Souls on November 1 and 2 honor the profound legacy of wisdom our ancestors have left to us. These feasts coincide with the Celtic feast of Samhain, which marks the beginning of the dark half of the year in the northern hemisphere and is a festival of the final harvest and remembering the dead. These moments on the great turning of the year's wheel are believed to be a "thin place" where the ancestors are especially accessible to us across the veil.

Psychologist Carl Jung wrote extensively about the collective unconscious which is this vast pool of ancestral memory within each of us. It is a kind of deposit of ancestral experience. He believed it comprises the psychic life of our ancestors right back to the earliest beginnings. Nothing is lost. All of the stories, struggles, and wisdom are available to us.

Each of us is an unconscious carrier of this ancestral experience and part of our journey is to bring this to consciousness in our lives. . . . The stories of our ancestors are woven into the fabric of our very being.

Gathering the Strength of the Ancestors

During a quiet, reflective period:
Recall a personal experience of your life when you faced a difficult situation. Remember how your inner strength helped you move through it. You have that strength residing in you now, the strength of the ancestors.

Write the names of deceased persons you have known (or people from literature, history, scripture, spirituality) whose strength has been passed on to you in some way. Think about their positive qualities and virtues (courage, sense of humor, ability to forgive, leadership, unselfishness, integrity, hospitality, etc.) List the names of five persons. When finished, unite quietly with them in gratitude. Pray to receive strength to enliven their qualities in your daily living.

Honoring the Strength of the Ancestors

A basket of medium-sized stones is passed around. Each person chooses one to hold. These stones represent the ancestral gift of strength. The group stands in a circle. As the stones are held, the names of the ancestors are proclaimed in the following way.

Each person speaks the name of one ancestor. After each name is spoken, all respond: **Guide us and grant us your strength.** *Continue going around the circle for five rounds, until all names are spoken.*

Closing Prayer

Leader: Beloved ancestors, your presence stretches back through the ages. It touches and influences the deep part of each of us today. Your strength sings in our spirits. Your courage abides in our hearts. Your resilience resonates in our bones. Your love abounds in our souls.

May we remember how connected we are to these enduring qualities. We offer gratitude for how the best of you continues to find life in us. Amen.

Song

"Wanting Memories," Sweet Honey in the Rock.

Celebrations

ANNIVERSARY OF ORDINATION

Jesus was a big toucher,
the New Testament has fourteen accounts
of him reaching out to touch another person,
often with healing, always with compassion.
—Patrick McCormick

The ordained stands, hands outstretched, palms up.

Leader: _____, these hands of yours are expressions of both the reality and the symbol of the years of that you have been living your ordination. When your hands were consecrated and anointed for service, you took this blessing seriously. As we bless your hands, we do so with immense gratitude for the quality of your person and your ministry. We remember how you have been a gift to the people gathered here, and to those who cannot be here, all those lives you have touched with the goodness of Christ.

Those present say after each blessing: **May the blessing of God enfold you.**

We bless your hands that formed the sign of the cross so many times . . .
We bless your hands that put the Bread of Life in countless other hands . . .
We bless your hands that embraced people consumed with grief . . .
We bless your hands that sent a caring note or a message of affirmation . . .
We bless your hands that created enriching and inspiring homilies . . .
We bless your hands that reached out in welcome to shake another's . . .
We bless your hands that drove your car to visit the sick and comfort the dying . . .
We bless your hands that wiped tears of compassion from your eyes . . .
We bless your hands that clapped in gratitude and affirmation . . .
We bless your hands that administered the sacrament of the sick . . .
We bless your hands that held the books you've read for personal growth . . .
We bless your hands that baptized and hallowed those being married . . .
We bless your hands that raised the cross in a Good Friday liturgy . . .
We bless your hands that gave a sign of forgiveness to a penitent . . .
We bless your hands that shared a meal at the table of friendship . . .

We bless your hands that held a phone as you listened to someone in need . . .

We bless your hands that greeted those coming for counseling . . .

We bless your hands that folded in daily meditation and personal prayer . . .

Leader: Together we pray:

May you go forward this day with faith knowing your hard work and endless efforts have enriched and helped those you served. Each time you look at your hands may you find a reason to hope, remembering all the good they have done. May the blessing of the Holy One enfold you and enhance your life with our gratitude and respect. Amen.

Birthday Meditation: Flower Garden Path

~⁀

Visualize yourself in a peaceful, colorful flower garden. Wide paths lined with blooming plants meander through the hidden glen. This garden full of blooms contains hints of the year ahead of you.

As you enter the garden, a divine companion comes to walk with you in this lovely place, reaching out to hold your hand. The two of you walk slowly, quietly, absorbing the fragrance and loveliness of the flourishing garden.

As you amble along you become aware that certain flowers have a message for you about another year of your life. You turn to inquire about this at the very moment your divine companion leans over, chooses a flower symbolizing *love of self and others*, and hands it to you.

You continue your slow pace, relishing the stillness and bliss within you. As you pass a plant with thick, robust stems, your companion carefully picks one of its flowers and hands it to you. This one represents *Courage* to grow and endure.

Now your companion finds a stem with several blooms on it, symbolizing *Peace—peace of mind, peace of heart, peace for the world*. Reach forth and accept this flower, too.

Turning a bend on the garden path, you come to a tall flower that characterizes *Faith*. You add this gift to your bouquet when it is held out to you.

There are several other flowers meant for you. Continue to walk in the lovely flower garden and see which ones your divine companion offers to you. Receive those flowers, as well.

You sit down now on a bench with your companion and hold the bouquet of flowers near your heart. You say a prayer of thanksgiving for what you have been offered as you begin another year of life.

When you are ready, tuck the flowers in a safe place in your heart, take your companion with you, rise up, and move out of the garden. Continue onward to celebrate the gift of your birth-day.

BIRTHDAY REFLECTION:
STORIES IN THE RIPPLES

Lake Vermillion with its wide cove
on far end of the north shore,
the constant, small ripples of water
splashing against the rocks,
each miniature wave carrying a story,
some from the ancient glaciers
and some from this present age of mine.
The rain-swollen clouds hold our tales of life,
and drop them into the expansive lake
year after year, absorbing
them into the one Great Story.

Today the ripples invite me to listen intently,
to find within them my own narrative:
the womb-like waters of a nine month gestation,
the gush and push of a small, unknown self
into a world that has grown me
into the person I now think I am.

And who am I? Still a ripple,
mostly composed of water.
Still full of story. Still trying
to tell myself and the world
who I believe I am, who I have become,
and who I wonder I will be
when the story of my watery self
slips forever into the Eternal Waters—

where all the ripples are one.

BLESSING FOR MOTHERS

One springtime I kept finding strings of dried grass and small twigs on the front porch. I solved this mystery by discovering an industrious mother robin building a nest behind the security light. During that same week I was immersed in the novel *The Twelve Tribes of Hattie*, the story of another industrious mother. Hattie worked tirelessly to feed and clothe her many children in extreme poverty (due to a womanizing, gambling husband). Hattie loved her children fiercely but lacked an ability to show them physical or verbal affection.

So many kinds of mothers exist in our world. Each has her own way of being with her children. In the United States we celebrate Mother's Day in May. While I honor the beautiful relationship I had with my birth mother, I think of both young and adult children with tenuous or difficult maternal relationships. Yet, no matter how this relationship is or has been, each mother gives her child the gift of life and the possibility of a worthy future.

A Blessing of Body, Mind, and Spirit for Mothers of All Sorts, Sizes, and Shapes

O mothers, one and all, some of you have carried your children in your womb. Others of you have welcomed babes in need of your attention who came to you from another birth mother. May the love you've poured forth return to you in plenitude.

O mothers, do not live in regret of what you wished you would have done, or what you did do and wished you had not. As you look back on your mothering, may you remember that you tried to do your best, given the circumstances.

O mothers, those of you for whom much of your life with your children is before you, do not imagine you can do this alone. Remember it takes a lot of leaning on the Divine Mother whose heart enfolds every mother and child. May you draw strength daily from her kindly sustenance.

O mothers, do not forget to care for yourself. Find what enriches and gladdens your heart. Be good to your body and spirit. Remember you are worthy of care and attention. May you have the vitality it takes to give generously of yourself.

O mothers, you who have gone on to another sphere of life, we welcome our memories of you and remember how much you mean to us. May the peace you now have flow into the weary and troubled hearts of mothers everywhere.

O mothers, for the countless times your hard work and generous self-giving was never thanked or acknowledged, was rejected or taken for granted, may you know yourself loved and appreciated today.

O mothers, we call today on the Divine Mother to draw you to her spacious heart, to replenish what needs revitalization in you. May you know her comfort, peace, and tender embrace. May you hear the Divine Mother's song of love humming in you. Amen.

A LITANY OF FATHERS EVERYWHERE

Pause after each group of fathers. Unite with the ones who are mentioned, remembering we are one in spirit; draw forth loving kindness from your heart and send it forth to these fathers. After each segment of named fathers, pray the following:

Heavenly Father, we bring our prayers for these earthly fathers to you.

Fathers holding a newly birthed child . . .
Fathers embracing a sick child . . .
Fathers counseling a wild child . . .
Fathers blessing every child . . .
Pause and pray:

Heavenly Father, we bring our prayers for these earthly fathers to you.

Weary fathers . . .
Depressed fathers . . .
Hungry fathers . . .
Happy fathers . . .
Pause and pray.

Fathers in offices . . .
Fathers at home . . .
Fathers in prosperity . . .
Fathers in poverty . . .
Pause and pray.

Homeless fathers . . .
Angry fathers . . .
Tender fathers . . .
Caring fathers . . .
Pause and pray.

Fathers who abuse . . .
Fathers who kill . . .
Fathers who weep . . .

Fathers who laugh . . .
Pause and pray.

Inconsiderate fathers . . .
Hard-hearted fathers . . .
Soft-hearted fathers . . .
Faith-filled fathers . . .
Pause and pray.

Fathers who stay . . .
Fathers who leave . . .
Fathers who hope . . .
Fathers who pray . . .
Pause and pray.

Energetic fathers . . .
Hard-working fathers . . .
Imprisoned fathers . . .
Traumatized fathers . . .
Pause and pray.

Trusted fathers . . .
Reckless fathers . . .
Addicted fathers . . .
Helpful fathers . . .
Pause and pray.

Fathers who produced life . . .
Fathers who instilled confidence . . .
Fathers who nurtured faith . . .
Fathers who never gave up . . .
Pause and pray

Fathers who long to be loved . . .
Fathers who never stop loving . . .
Fathers who are deceased . . .
Fathers who are a blessing . . .
Pause and pray.

Other fathers we want to mention *(voice these names)* . . .

*A*ll: We celebrate you, fathers of our world, fathers of our lives. We pray you will receive the strength and renewed dedication that Jesus found in his mountainside solitude as he sojourned with his Father. May all you have given from the generosity of your love be returned to you a hundredfold and more. Peace be yours, peace, peace, peace.

Valentine's Day: A Litany of Hearts

Let us pray this Valentine's Day that

broken hearts be mended
young hearts stay wonder-filled
old hearts discover their wisdom
embittered hearts let go of hurt
compassionate hearts find strength
big hearts know their wealth
betrayed hearts recover trust
soft hearts not be wounded
hardened hearts begin to soften
sensitive hearts be vigilant
happy hearts announce their joy
courageous hearts keep risking
passionate hearts tend the flames
arrogant hearts learn humility
sympathetic hearts benefit others
determined hearts lessen their grip
jealous hearts accept what they have
lost hearts find their way home
loving hearts reach out to others
generous hearts receive in return
fearful hearts turn toward trust
empty hearts befriend loneliness
tepid hearts stretch into action
faithful hearts remain steadfast

Kindhearted Holy One, you gather all these hearts into your one great love. Thank you for reaching our heart through the hearts of others. The genuine love of each person reflects your divine affection. Keep us aware, when we hesitate or question our ability to share our love with another, that you dwell within our hearts. Amen.

A Litany of Mothers Everywhere

~

Pause after each group of women. Unite with the mothers mentioned, remembering we are one in spirit; draw forth loving kindness from your heart and send it forth to these women. After each segment of named mothers, pray the following:

Divine Mother, we bring our prayers for these earthly mothers to you.

First-time mothers . . .
Grandmothers . . .
Motherless mothers . . .
Faith-filled mothers . . .
Pause and pray:

Divine Mother, we bring our prayers for these earthly mothers to you.

Mothers of poor and hungry children . . .
Mothers of orphaned and abandoned ones . . .
Mothers of disabled and bullied youth . . .
Mothers of child soldiers and sex slaves . . .
Pause and pray.

Educated mothers . . .
Illiterate mothers . . .
Cherished mothers . . .
Taken-for-granted mothers . . .
Pause and pray.

Compassionate mothers . . .
Nursing mothers . . .
Courageous mothers . . .
Laughing mothers . . .
Pause and pray.

Incarcerated mothers . . .
Drug addicted mothers . . .
Prostituted mothers . . .

Raped mothers . . .
Pause and pray.

Mothers who speak out for justice . . .
Mothers who read to their children . . .
Mothers who sing in the shower . . .
Mothers who linger to look at the moon . . .
Pause and pray.

Mothers of the disappeared . . .
Mothers of those killed or maimed in war . . .
Mothers of run-away teenagers . . .
Mothers of children who take their lives . . .
Pause and pray.

Unhappy mothers . . .
Homeless mothers . . .
Battered mothers . . .
Refugee mothers . . .
Pause and pray.

Mothers in nursing homes . . .
Mothers in struggling marriages . . .
Mothers in difficult work situations . . .
Mothers in financial difficulty . . .
Pause and pray.

Lesbian mothers . . .
Non-biological mothers . . .
Single mothers . . .
Divorced mothers . . .
Pause and pray.

Mothers who long to be loved . . .
Mothers who never stop loving . . .
Mothers who are deceased . . .
Mothers who are a blessing . . .
Pause and pray.

Other mothers we want to mention *(voice these names)* . . .

*A*ll: We celebrate you, mothers of our world, mothers of our lives. You are cradled in the arms of the Great Mother. Be nurtured and nestled in the spiritual womb of this renewing love. May all that you have given for the sake of others be returned to you a hundredfold and more. Peace be yours, peace, peace, peace.

Spring Equinox Rejoicing

Our planet tilts toward the sun.
Stronger sunlight, and more of it,
warms our days and our spirits.
Let us rejoice!

The winter snow melts away.
Brown, gray sludge is rinsed off
from sidewalks and streets
by the cleansing rainfalls.
Let us rejoice!

Green shoots push their way up
from the once frozen, hardened soil.
They have survived the winter
and announce their aliveness.
Let us rejoice!

Birdsongs fill the air with melody.
They sing to their future mates
with the hope of attracting love
and having little birds fill their nests.
Let us rejoice!

Creatures asleep in their lairs
yawn and stretch
from their long winter slumber.
They are ready now to rejoin life.
Let us rejoice!

The woods welcome tiny flowers
and the first hints of green leaves.
Crocuses show their faces,
and promise more color to come.
Let us rejoice!

Geese heading north
honk their traveler's greeting
as they sail their way home
on the wings of March wind.
Let us rejoice!

Seeds that fell from wild plants
and hid themselves under leaves
now take root and begin to grow,
a signal of earth's resurrection.
Let us rejoice!

Children's voices echo in play,
their hearty laughter
drawing all who hear them
into heartfelt happiness.
Let us rejoice!

People everywhere taste the freshness
of Spring's brand new arrival.
Their grumpiness lessens
and their hearts grow lighter and freer.
Let us rejoice!

St. Patrick's Day

Namasté. I greet the place in you where heaven and earth meet.

Introduction: from "This Place That Has Made Us Kin," an interview with Barbara Brown Taylor published in *Flycatcher Journal*

Leader: I've known thin places all my life, but I didn't have the language for them until I took a trip to Ireland a few years back. . . . Thin places are transparent places or moments, set apart by the quality of the sunlight in them, or the shadows, or the silence, or the sounds—see how many variations there are? What they have in common is their luminosity, the way they light an opening between this world and another—I'd say "between this world and the next," but that makes it sound like one world has to end before the next one can begin, and a thin place doesn't work like that. It works to make you more aware of the thin veil between apparent reality and deeper reality. It works to pull aside the veil for just a moment, so you can see through.

Sometimes I know I'm in a thin place because it feels like the floor just dropped two or three levels beneath my feet and set me down in a deeper place. They can open up just about anywhere. . . . But thin places aren't always lovely places, and they're not always outdoors. Hospital rooms can be thin places. So can emergency rooms and jail cells. A thin place is any place that drops you down to where you know you're in the presence of the Really Real—the Most Real—God, if you insist.

Song

"Shekinah," *Holy Ground*, Monica Brown.

Reading: Genesis 28:10–22

Surely the Lord is in this place—and I did not know it.

> *Quiet time to ponder our own experiences of thin places.*
> *Sharing of Thin Place Experiences*

Prayer of Gratitude for Thin Places

Leader: Divine Guest, present to us especially in our "thin veil" moments, we pause to pray:

> Thank you for the quickening of our hearts, the silencing of our words, when we briefly know that you are "in this place."
>
> Thank you for those experiences when nature draws us into a memorable awareness of your awesome presence.
>
> Thank you for the unexpected and profound realization of our communion with you through other human beings.
>
> Thank you for Earth's creatures' leading us into a realm of unspoken attentiveness to your life moving through all of us.
>
> Thank you for the brief, but forever remembered, felt unity with you during a time of individual or communal prayer.
>
> Thank you for the generous kindness of another person awakening our heart to your intimate nearness.
>
> Thank you for the upsurge of joy when a freshly birthed child utters the first cry, your breath instilling life in another human being.
>
> Thank you for the felt mystery of your enduring, eternal love in the mortal space of the dying.
>
> Thank you for the leap into light that surprisingly lifts our darkened spirits from their closets of melancholy.
>
> Thank you for those times the thin veil between us parted and we knew your love inseparable from our own.

Prayer

Together: Holy Mystery, we come to an awareness of how close you are to us when we are swept into a place of "knowing" that lies beyond our rational control. Today we remember and bring our gratitude for those quickly fleeting glimpses of our deep and strong unity with you. We turn again to draw strength from the unexplainable sureness of your abiding love. Remind us of this glimpse on the days when our minds and hearts seem far from you. Wrap us in the memories of our thin places when we knew without hesitation that we were one with you.

Song

"Deep Peace," *By Breath*, Sara Thomsen.

Compassion

Canon of Hospitality

All Christians are called to be hospitable,
But it is more than serving a meal or filling a bed,
opening our door—it is to open ourselves,
our hearts, to the needs of others.
Hospitality is not just shelter,
but the quality of welcome behind it.
—Dorothy Day

As we gather around the table of friendship
we come with profound thanksgiving
for the countless times
we have been welcomed by the Holy One
dwelling in another person.
Because of open minds and loving hearts
we have been received with warmth and kindness.

All: **Come in. Come in. Come in, I welcome you. God is here.**

We bring our sorrow and ask forgiveness
for the times we have ignored, shunned,
or deliberately refused to welcome others.
We bring our intention to continue our efforts
to accept those with whom we have differences.

All: **Come in. Come in. Come in, I welcome you. God is here.**

We welcome those who claim to be our enemies.
We welcome those who thwart our attempts at caring.
We welcome those whose demeanor frightens us.
We welcome those whose beliefs and lifestyles
appear contrary to those of our own.
We welcome those who live among us
whom we would rather not welcome.

All: **Come in. Come in. Come in, I welcome you. God is here.**

We are grateful for biblical compassionate persons
renowned for their all-embracing hospitality.
Their generous welcome inspires and encourages
our own welcoming of those most in need
of food, clothing, lodging, and visitation.

All: **Come in. Come in. Come in, I welcome you. God is here.**

We are especially grateful for the example
of Abraham and Sarah who received strangers,
Pharaoh's daughter who brought Moses to her home,
Elizabeth who greeted Mary of Nazareth with joy,
Lydia of Philippi who offered hospitality to the disciples,
and Mary, Martha, and Lazarus of Bethany
in whose home Jesus found the gift of friendship.

All: **Come in. Come in. Come in, I welcome you. God is here.**

We pray to grow stronger and live more fully
the vital qualities of hospitality: kindness, non-judgment,
understanding, generosity, acceptance and good cheer.
When our time and presence is required in welcoming others
may we do so without grumbling or regret.

All: **Come in. Come in. Come in, I welcome you. God is here**.

We remember the two on the road to Emmaus
who were welcomed by the risen Christ.
He drew them close with compassion
and lifted their spirits with kindness.
As they sat at table in the breaking of bread
their disappointed hearts began to heal.

All: **Come in. Come in. Come in, I welcome you. God is here.**

COURAGE AND COMPASSION

Ponder where your courage and compassion reside. Pray for these virtues to be fortified.

I pray to have courage and compassion to:

> be faithful to a spiritual practice even when constant duties lure me away from it;
>
> resist a response that blames an underprivileged group for the injustice they experience;
>
> persist in clearing my heart of its emotional armor and tendency toward building walls;
>
> recover self-worth after being maligned by another's harsh treatment;
>
> change my biases, prejudices, and baseless views about other religious beliefs;
>
> cultivate an open mind and heart toward those I am inclined to quickly dismiss;
>
> go beyond mere acceptance and enter into relationship with people of diversity;
>
> speak up for those who do not have the power or means to speak for themselves;
>
> choose to live with fewer material possessions so others' basic needs are met;
>
> enter into dialogue when angry differences and misunderstandings create division;
>
> refuse to harbor thoughts and feelings of revenge and retaliation toward anyone;

cultivate a spirit of gratitude and eliminate entitlement from my expectations;

accept my deficiencies and allow them to teach me about being compassionate;

step out of my tight schedule and choose to be a caring presence with someone;

unclench and release my strong opinions until they drop out of my padlocked grasp;

re-gather my hope for people's well-being when their situations look dismal;

focus my wandering mind and listen with full attentiveness to others;

stand on a firm foundation of prayer and approach all persons with compassion.

GRATITUDE FOR COMPASSIONATE PRESENCE

Compassionate One, the amount of suffering in our world appears to be insurmountable, but the amount of kindheartedness is equally vast. It is easy to forget this. Let us give thanks for those who embody your love and let us be willing to share it.

We are grateful for

persons who dedicate their livelihood to alleviate suffering in any form;

researchers in science, medicine, psychology, and other disciplines who study aspects of compassion related to the suffering of body, mind, and spirit;

directors, staff members, and participants of programs worldwide who focus on developing compassionate presence and altruistic action to alleviate suffering;

leaders of religion who both preach and live the tenets of a compassionate life;

teachers, parents, daycare providers, staff at youth rehabilitation centers, and all who interact with children in a respectful and reverent manner;

those who tirelessly minister to lonely, homeless, forgotten, imprisoned, war-wearied, immigrated, prostituted, and other marginalized individuals;

politicians and government leaders who consistently keep the needs of suffering people as one of their basic guidelines in decision-making;

persons who recognize and tend to the concerns of Earth's creatures and natural world;

children whose generosity and sensitive concern for disenfranchised people leads them to reach out with acts of compassion;

wounded ones whose spirit is loving and large enough to offer forgiveness to those who have hurt them;

the countless men and women whose daily efforts to ease the suffering of others goes unnoticed, but makes a significant difference for people with mental, emotional, physical, and spiritual distress.

*C*ompassionate One, you hear the cries of the world; we are grateful to you for showing us how to be with those who suffer. Thank you for your bountiful kindness offered to our world through people of selfless endeavor. How grateful we are that we can join them in being your loving heart and hands. We go forth with expanded gratitude and renewed inspiration to be a compassionate presence. Amen.

PRAYER FOR PEACE

Stand at a window, preferably facing east—the place of sunrise, the direction of hope. If you do not have a window, stand in an open doorway.

Send peace to your loved ones.

Place your hands over your heart. Move your attention toward your inner being. Slowly move inward until you reach that place deep inside of you where abiding peace dwells, the core of enduring love.

Now allow your attention to move toward your loved ones. Recall their presence in your life. Open your hands and extend them outward, palms up. Send forth peace from your heart to those you love, especially those not in harmony with themselves or others.

Send peace to the suffering ones of the world.

Place your hands again over your heart. Move your attention toward your inner being. Slowly move inward again until you reach that place deep inside of you where abiding peace dwells, the core of enduring love.

Bring to mind the suffering ones of our world, especially those who live in fear of being harmed in any way. Open your hands and extend them outward, palms up. Send forth the deep peace in the center of your being to these suffering ones.

Send peace to those whom you find difficult to accept.

Place your hands again over your heart. Move your attention toward your inner being. Once more, slowly move inward until you reach that place deep inside of you where abiding peace dwells, the core of enduring love.

Bring to mind those whose presence, personality, ideas, attitudes, or actions create judgmental, hostile, or irritating feelings within you. Focus on one particular person or a group of people who challenge your ability to love. Open your hands and extend them outward, palms up. With as much true intention as will arise within you, send forth the deep peace in the center of your being to this person or group.

Send peace to those who consider you their enemy.

Place your hands again over your heart. Move your attention toward your inner being. Slowly move further inward until you reach that place deep inside of you where abiding peace dwells.

Bring to mind those known or unknown who consider you an enemy. Open your hands and extend them outward, palms up. With as much true intention as will arise within you, send forth the deep peace in the center of your being to those who consider you their enemy.

Send peace to your self.

Place your hands again over your heart. Move your attention toward your inner being. Slowly move further inward until you reach that place deep inside of you where abiding peace dwells.

Turn toward yourself. Ponder how you view yourself and your current situation. Allow any area of concern, hurt, or worry to arise. Hold one hand over your heart and extend the other hand on top of your head. Send forth love from your heart to your self. Receive this love as fully as you can.

Concluding Prayer

Peace-Bringer, create in me a heart filled with the kind of love that reflects your own. Send this love to those I care about and respect. Open my mind to those I want to reject. Open my heart to those I prefer to avoid. Open my eyes to see beyond the surface of individuals and recognize your presence in each one. May my thoughts, words, and deeds be devoid of violence in any form. Soften whatever is hardened in my heart so that I bring your peace wherever I go. Remind me often that I, too, am in need of this love and worthy to receive it.

Difficult Times

A PRAYER FOR STRENGTH

For God alone my soul waits in silence.
[God] alone is my rock and my salvation, my fortress;
I shall never be shaken.
—Psalm 62:1a, 2

Rock and Refuge, Stronghold of Souls, Unshakeable One,
infuse your strength into the places where I feel the greatest weakness.
Permeate the parts of my life that continually challenge my patience.
Increase an ability to accept those who seem to be most unacceptable.
Lessen any tendency in my spirit that gives way to a loss of hope.
Reinforce an awareness of the daily manifestations of your presence.
Boost my spirit when I think I cannot manage what is mine to be and do.

Provider of Purpose, Firm Foundation, Enduring Love,
support my determination to give the best of my self to others.
Fortify the forgiveness you have placed and nurtured in my heart.
Sustain a solid belief that I can get through what appears insurmountable.
Bolster my efforts to be a person who reaches out to those who suffer.
Foster greater trust in you when worries and anxieties attempt to prevail.
Impart the courage I need to change what appears to be unchangeable.

In you I find sufficient strength, abounding love, and secure serenity.

An Ember Still Aglow

In her poem in *The Art of Resilience* Carol Orsborn refers to the defeating experiences that inevitably make their way into our lives. She wisely proposes that when these downward cycles happen to us, we may feel like only "charred wood" remains. Orsborn urges the reader to poke around those ashes and find an ember that still has the ability to spark restored fire when it is tended with "love and hope."

I found immense encouragement when I came across this hope-filled poem. Like most people, I have known those times of "charred wood." I needed to be reminded that something new could resurrect after a destructive experience. The following reflection offers an opportunity to remember those "charred wood" times in your life, and to acknowledge the embers that eventually found flame and brought new vitality.

We recall times when we received painful, upsetting news, how suddenly life took on the shape of unhappiness and apprehension.

We recall times of having to move on from something or someone harmful to our well-being.

We recall the darkness and uncertainty pressing upon our emotional and mental state when life was filled with unresolved issues.

We recall sadness and a sense of loss when we said farewell to persons, places, or things we considered to be of great value.

We recall being hammered down by ungrounded and unfair judgments in the words and deeds of others.

We recall emotional and mental distress that led us to think it would never release itself and allow us a happier future.

We recall standing beneath the cross of another in great need of our faithful companionship and tender caring.

We recall times of having an inordinate amount of suffering placed in the lap of our lives and being required to receive it.

We recall being offended and becoming vulnerable, learning patience and humility through those hurts.

We recall how we made it through what seemed to be impossibly difficult and tumultuous times.

We recall the slow yet steady turn toward hope after the blows of defeat and disaster turned our world upside down.

We recall the fleeting moments when we sensed a power greater than ourselves at work amid the harshness that surrounded us.

We recall the unexpected tenderness, the startling kindness, the warmth of acceptance that breathed on the embers of our heart when we most needed to believe the fire was still there.

Ceaseless Ember, the steady glow of your strengthening love never dies. You breathe on the barely-alive ashes of what seems to be the destruction of our hope. You stay with us, a spark of love within our discontent. You slowly ignite our spirits with restored confidence and belief in a less turbulent future. May we remember this when life does not go as we wish. Amen.

Laying Down My Burdens

Cross-bearer and Wearer of the Wood,
many are the burdens that press with force
upon my spirit as I trudge through life.
These cares and concerns weigh heavily,
pushing their energy upon both mind and heart,
taking their toll, lessening my power to love well.
These burdens shape themselves into leaden anchors
of growling self-pity and loss of self-confidence.
They snatch away joy and destroy empathy.
Today I choose to release their useless weight.
I am ready to stop dragging them alongside me.
Here are my troubles, struggles, and afflictions.
I lay them down before your cross. I let them go.
I undo the clutching of shame, guilt, and blame.
I step back from painful patterns of the past
that leak into my current thinking and behavior.
I do not need to drag down my life under the bulk
of these needless burdens bearing weight on me.
I deliberately move on with fresh freedom,
placing faith in your strength and compassion.
I leave my burdens here with you today.
I will not take them back.

The Peace of the Life-Giver Be With You

Blessed are they who put their strength in You.
They do not give way to fear or doubt;
they are quickened by divine light and power.
—Psalm 84 (Nan C. Merrill)

Meditation

Breathe in calmness.
Breathe out anxiety and lack of peace.
Sojourn with confidence in the Holy One's company.

Blessing

Response to each: **I rest in the Peace-Giver's presence.**
When inner turmoil and conflict threaten my peace of mind and heart . . .
When my life is overly full and I wonder how I will complete what is required . . .
When I enter into the pain and the suffering of the world's lack of peace . . .
When I hurt for friends, relatives, and others who are distressed . . .
When fear of the future rises up and the way ahead is uncertain and unsettled . . .
When my life appears empty and loneliness taunts me . . .
When I live with concern and apprehension over unresolved issues . . .
When I feel a great distance from the One who is the fullness of peace . . .

Gracious Peace-Maker, thank you for the life you have given me. I desire to be filled with your serenity. Clothe me in your calm presence. Be the stronghold of my heart. Help me to accept the irreversible and to change what is possible. May your peace grow ever stronger in me.

SENTINEL OF STRENGTH

God is closer to us than our own soul,
for God is the foundation on which the soul stands.
Our soul sits in God and in true rest,
and our soul stands in God in sure strength,
and our soul is naturally rooted in God's endless love.
—Julian of Norwich

The tall, thin cottonwood tree,
with its tattered autumn leaves
still attached to the battered branches,
stands alone by the side of Lake Michigan,
a landmark for the path to the shoreline.
But for myself, much more than that.
The tree reminds me of resiliency,
the long white line down its trunk,
a visible, split-open revelation of strength.

Healed now from severe lightning strike,
this naked exposure speaks to my need:
"Stand in your sorrow. Stand strong.
You can heal. Life chooses to go on.
Wounds leave their distinct scars
but that is not the end of the story.
Your value continues to thrive
in your imperfect, wounded state.
You, too, serve a significant purpose,
a sentinel of enduring strength,
a new power stored in your memory,
whispering hope when your heart
wants to whither in its unhappiness."

Easter

EASTER RENEWAL OF JOY

Risen Jesus, assure me of the promised joy implicit in your risen life.

Reenergize my spirit when it creeps into the cave of gloom. Bring it forth into the light of your radiance.

Reestablish attentiveness to the wonder found in nature's continual unfolding of the seasons, each one with its own inherent beauty.

Reinvigorate a desire to enter each day confident of your grace to maintain a positive perspective, no matter what unexpected turbulence or distress confronts me.

Renew an ability to find satisfaction in my faith without having to poke continually at truths that remain unresolved.

Resist my attempts to foster complete control, and thus I miss the adventure of risk-taking and the invitation to step out of tightly bound securities.

Reclaim love grown cold or dormant due to neglect, misperception, or the deluge of overwork that quickly steals affection from my heart.

Restore order and balance in my mind. Clear it of tangling thoughts, judgments, and issues that stealthily poison my enjoyment of life.

Resurrect the undivided passion I once had for bringing the best of my inner goodness to each and every part of what claims my attention.

Reveal what keeps playfulness from emerging, forfeiting the freedom to express the laughter hiding inside of me.

Release the door of my heart to let me enter the tender moments and unforeseen experiences holding great happiness if only I am open to them.

*C*reator of Joy, lift out of my heart any heaviness or deadly doldrums residing there. Turn my attention toward opportunities to rejoice: the colors, shapes, and sounds of beauty my eyes and ears unconsciously see and hear, unexpected kindness, the dawning of each new day, the quiet approaching of night, and all those little lifts of joy I can quickly pass by without noticing or offering thanks. Reach me with your Eastering joy and tuck me happily into your ever-present gladness. Amen.

GREAT TRAVELER

Great Traveler,
you beguile two crestfallen disciples
on the road to Emmaus;
you draw them in
with your arrowed questions,
urge them to turn the story over,
to recall each piece of it,
although you already know
the disturbing memory.
You speak your golden words,
softening the travelers' sadness,
revealing what their hearts
yearn to believe: life thrives beyond death.
Slowly their sagging spirits rouse
with recognition, allured by the faint scent
of your prevailing presence.

"Stay! Stay! Stay with us!"
And you do.

You break bread with them,
and when the lamp of love
flames high, you rise quietly
and gently slip away.

Joy washes over past bewilderment,
propels the disciples outward.
They go, carrying a taste of love,
a voice of hope, a word of comfort
to those waiting in the wounded harbor
of disbelief.

Now, after the closeness of prayer,
I, too, go out,
carrying the flaming heart of communion,

go to embrace you, the Great Traveler,
through the integrity of my life,

go to carry the lighted lamp of Love in me,
out and beyond, into the heart of a world
where the same Lamp shines vividly
for all to see.

HOLY SATURDAY

What happened in the tomb, that darkened space
between the Cross and the noiseless linens laid aside?
Who speaks to us of this inaudible obscurity?
No one. The secret of silent gestation overlooked
in favor of the grand moment of resurrection. And yet,
a part of each life bears resemblance to that bleakness
in which a quiet turning from death to life unfolds.

A similar story of the unheard, the unspoken, the unfelt
breathes in the wintered bud preparing for blossom,
the caterpillar cells giving way to a monarch's beauty,
the wonder of a human forming in a mother's womb,
a sleeping seed awakening in the darkened soil.

Each turns slowly toward life, like the Beloved of the Soul
tethered by thickness of stone in the tomb's seclusion.
There the Holy One waited, coming forth as all-abiding Spirit,
forever present, forever near, forever in love with us.

Who urges us to sit still, to be patient in the nurturing tomb
of darkness, to enter its enveloping silence with assurance?
Where do we seek steady courage when sadness, distress,
confusion, and flatness wall us in with airless depression?
How do we wait with a balance of acceptance and yearning,
relinquishment and action, hesitation and confidence?

The stones that block our light, whatever they might be—
let us stop shoving them aside. Give ourselves over
to the gestation required before hope's fresh air unseals the tomb.

Do not hurry the soul's metamorphosis. Trust in the maturation
of some essential growth. Remain confident. Keep focused
on the Risen One. Breathe in the possibility of some new joy,
for it hides in this very moment, readying itself to slip past the stone.

HOPE

Always be ready to make your defense
to anyone who demands from you
an accounting for hope that is in you;
yet do it with gentleness and reverence.
                                    —1 Peter 3:15–16

Reading: from *An Interrupted Life*, Etty Hillisum

(Etty Hillisum, a young Dutch, Jewish woman, lived at the time of the Holocaust. Her diaries and letters tell of remarkable spiritual growth during the Nazi occupation. She died at Auschwitz in 1943 at age twenty-nine.)

My battles are fought out inside, with my own demons; it is not in my nature to tilt against the savage, cold-blooded fanatics who clamor for our destruction. I am not afraid of them either, I don't know why; I am so calm it is sometimes as if I were standing on the parapets of the palace of history looking down over far-distant lands. This bit of history we are experiencing right now is something I know I can stand up to. I know what is happening, and yet my head is clear. But sometimes I feel as if a layer of ashes were being sprinkled over my heart, as if my face were withering and decaying before my very eyes, and as if everything were falling apart in front of me and my heart were letting go. But these are brief moments; then everything falls back into place, my head is clear again, and I can once more bear and stand up to this piece of history that is ours. For once you have begun to walk with God, you need only keep on walking with Him and all of life becomes one long stroll—such a marvelous feeling.

Meditation

Begin by recalling the gift of hope that the risen Jesus brought to each person who experienced his presence when he moved among them after being raised from the dead.

No matter how you are emotionally, mentally, physically,
Invite hope into your life.
Allow hope to enter into your mind.
Allow hope to enter into your spirit.
Allow hope to enter into your body.
Allow yourself to be filled with hope.

Imagine the Spirit of Jesus stirring up newness,
finding the dead places that exist within your spirit,
and creating a meadow of flowers inside of you.
Visualize this open space, the flower buds unfolding,
filling the spacious meadow with color and fragrance.

Let hope fill your mind with a sense of purpose and direction.
Let hope fill your spirit with life and enthusiasm.
Let hope fill your heart and draw you into renewed love.

Rest quietly in your restored hope.
Let the power of Risen Love reign in your heart.

Extending Hope to the World

Bring to mind people in the world who are especially in need of hope, both
those you know personally and those whose names are unknown to you, especially people who are grieving, living in poverty, imprisoned unjustly, isolated
because of illness or aging, held in refugee camps, victims of violence and all
forms of abuse, depressed or suffering from mental illness, and any others
whose hope may have grown frail.

Turn toward the depths of hope that you recalled in your deepest self.
With each person or group of people who arise in your mind, offer hope from
your heart to them. You might imagine yourself gently embracing the other
in silence, or holding out a blossoming flower, or sitting side by side quietly
holding hands, or reaching forth with a look of love, or offering Eucharist or
a special blessing, or any other image that extends courage, strength, and an
invitation for a peaceful mind and heart.

Commitment to Hope

Invite the Spirit of the Risen Jesus to assist you in maintaining trust and confidence. Recommit yourself to living with hope, the kind that flows out from you into transforming love. You might want to write this commitment and read it each morning of the Easter season. Follow the reading of the commitment by once again extending hope to those most in need.

Spiritual Gestation

Each year when the feast of Easter arrives, I question if Christians focus enough on the tomb-time. Most move quickly from Good Friday to Easter liturgies with nary a look at the Crucified One's sojourn in the tomb's liminal waiting period. This hurried move from death into life reflects Western culture's inability to remain long with hurt and distress, seeking quick alleviation and allowing little space for the darkness and mystery that grows one into a clearer, deeper way of living. The Risen One's tomb-time provides a powerful metaphor for this spiritual gestation. New life and hope spring forth from the Easter story only after Jesus' time of darkness and defeat. It is from this perspective that I offer the following Easter prayer.

Risen One, I turn to you as my model of spiritual growth. Open my entire being to your grace-filled presence. Teach me repeatedly how to enter into my own tomb-times.

Grant trust in my ability to abide in the tomb of indecision and uncertainty, those times when I encounter confusion and do not know where I am going or what might happen next.

Remind me of the need for patience when I want to hurry through the tomb of my sorrow, instead of acknowledging and tending to the unwelcome aspects of grief residing within me.

Give courage to enter the tomb of physical suffering, to find inner strength by uniting in kinship with your experience of bodily pain and the absence of relief.

Wrap your compassion around my own when I choose to reside in the tomb of the world's growing violence. Restore hope when my longings for global peace disappear from view.

Be the quiet whisper of anticipated liberation when the tomb of unshakeable discouragement robs me of my inherent gladness and enthusiasm for life.

Take my hand when I dwell in the tomb of identity transition and am unsure of who I am. Assure me that, no matter how I might change, you and I are united at the core of my being.

Breathe your love in me when I experience the tomb of relationship breakage so that I have the bigness of heart to forgive another and the confidence to keep on believing in myself.

Support me when I am in the tomb of doubt, and my questions of faith scare me. Confirm my trust that you know the intention of my heart to remain always faithful to you.

Keep my inner eye on your Easter Story so the promise of spiritual growth continues to live in my heart no matter how long or strong the tomb-time might be. May others who experience life's in-between periods of entombment be encouraged, knowing they will also eventually find their way beyond the darkness that engulfs them. Amen.

The Tomb of Resurrection

Items needed: plain white paper and washable markers

Invitation

The tomb of Good Friday with its thick boulder blocking air and light persists through Holy Saturday until it becomes the opened tomb of Easter. Now this tomb is empty of its occupant and filled with angelic radiance. The tomb that once smelled of death and destruction now stands as a witness to surprising restoration of life. We come to this tomb today, carrying the hope it signifies. We come knowing a part of us still has blocks to fullness of life that need to be removed. We also come recognizing the places within us where the Holy One has freed us from our loss, where joy and confidence have overcome our numbed responsiveness. Let us now proceed to enter into each of these tombs.

Reading 1: John 19:40–42

They took the body of Jesus and wrapped it with the spices in linen cloths, according to the burial custom of the Jews. Now there was a garden in the place where he was crucified, and in the garden there was a new tomb in which no one had ever been laid. And so, because it was the Jewish day of Preparation, and the tomb was nearby, they laid Jesus there.

> *Participants are invited to draw a tomb with a boulder or blockage at the entrance. (An alternative to this: provide papers with an image of this tomb.)*

Reflect on any external situation or internal aspect where you feel some part of your life or inner being is currently entombed, inert, unresponsive, seemingly dead or dormant.

What has kept your body, mind, and spirit from being free, inspired, and energized? Write words for this on the blocked entrance to the tomb.

> *Participants hold this paper in their hands during the following reading.*

Reading 2: John 20:1–2

Early on the first day of the week, while it was still dark, Mary Magdalene came to the tomb and saw that the stone had been removed from the tomb. So she ran and went to Simon Peter and the other disciple, the one whom Jesus loved, and said to them, "They have taken the Lord out of the tomb, and we do not know where they have laid him."

Participants now approach a bowl of water. They dip their papers with words for the blocked tomb into the water and observe the words being washed away. They then receive a second piece of paper and are invited to draw a tomb again, an open one with the stone rolled away. (An alternative to this: provide papers with a graphic of this tomb.)

Recall times when you felt new life and restored hope. Did this come about through an event, a prayer, a song, nature, a person, a book or some other way? Write words indicating your sources of hope on the opening of the tomb.

Following this, participants are invited to hold this paper in their hands while the leader prays the following affirmations.

Affirmations

Angels of the blocked tomb, stand guard over the parts of our lives that await being raised from the dead. Release any boulders holding us back so we can go forth to share our spiritual renewal after receiving it.

Mary of Magdala, with your experience as an inspiration, our yearning for the Divine Gardener will grow to be as true and strong as yours. May we become as devoted as you were so that we, too, meet and recognize the Holy One in the garden of our lives.

Spirit of the risen Christ, nurture our hope. Continue to lead us to experiences that roll away the stone of entombment. Be the radiance that lights our way. Guide us toward a life dedicated to loving unconditionally.

Turning toward the Risen Christ

Reading: John 20:16

Jesus said to her, "Mary." She turned and said to him in Hebrew, "Rabbouni!" (which means Teacher).

When Jesus appears to Mary of Magdala in the garden by the empty tomb, there are two significant turnings that move her from intense sorrow to surprising joy. After the angels ask Mary what brings her to the tomb she tells them of her sorrow. Then she "*turned* around and saw Jesus standing there, but she did not know that it was Jesus" (Jn 20:13). Jesus asks Mary why she is weeping and who she is looking for. Mary does not answer directly. Instead, she questions him about where the body has been taken, hoping to go and remove it. This is when the second turning occurs. "Jesus said to her, 'Mary!' She *turned* and said to him in Hebrew, 'Rabbouni!'(which means Teacher)."

Reflection

Twice Mary turns before recognizing the risen Christ. In our lives it may take a number of turnings, both inner and outer, before we recognize how intimately present this Beloved One is with us. In the following prayer we turn our bodies as well as our spirits toward the joy of the resurrection. We pray for those like Mary of Magdala who are in the garden of their sorrows and disturbances. We pray they will be encouraged by the Risen One to turn toward the hope and joy found in the Easter message.

Invitation to Turn

Imagine that you are where Mary of Magdala was, at the entrance to the opened tomb.

Pause to look within your life; visit the places that seek the gift of restoration that the empty tomb signifies.

Turn your heart now to the risen Christ. Hear him call your name. Open your entire self to receive what this beloved presence bestows to you. Let this offering rest confidently within you.

Prayer of Turning toward the Risen Christ

Stand, turn, and face east.

We turn to you, risen Christ, and pray:

    for those whose dreams have been shattered, may they turn toward restored hope,

    for those who have grown weary from constant turmoil, may they turn toward peace,

    for those who feel disheartened, may they turn toward a spirit of encouragement,

    for those who have stopped believing in happiness, may they turn toward a reason to rejoice.

Turn and face south.

We turn to you, risen Christ, and pray:

    for those who find little value in their work, may they turn toward fresh motivation,

    for those with faltering relationships, may they turn toward a disposition to love,

    for those whose outlook on life is bleak, may they turn toward a rekindling of joy,

    for those who lack self-worth, may they turn toward their imperishable goodness.

Turn and face west.

We turn to you, risen Christ, and pray:

    for those who are sorrowful, may they turn toward you and find renewed gladness,

    for those who suffer in body, mind, or spirit, may they turn toward healing,

    for those in challenging transitions, may they turn toward trust in your guidance,

    for those who have lost their inner direction, may they turn toward home.

Turn and face north.

We turn to you, risen Christ, and pray:

> for those troubled in their faith, may they turn toward confidence in your love,
>
> for those who feel burdened, may they turn toward reliance on your strength,
>
> for those seeking vengeance, may they turn toward a heartfelt desire to forgive,
>
> for those who doubt joy will ever arise, may they turn toward your resurrection.

Prayer

Together: Risen Christ, we turn to you with full reliance on your resurrected presence with us here and now. We renew our trust in your grace to restore our joy when it lies hidden in our entombed self. Turn us again and again toward hope. Open our hearts to recognize you in the garden of our everyday lives. Amen.

Grief and Loss

CLOSING OF THE CASKET

~

Though we need to weep your loss,
You dwell in that safe place in our hearts
Where no storm or night or pain can reach you.
—John O'Donohue

Hold one hand to your heart.

Remember the love uniting you with _____.
This love will never leave you. It is your strength today and always.
This love will keep you united to _____ as the future reveals itself.

Hold your hands out, palms up and open.

Receive the love and appreciation you have for _____.

Cover your heart with your hands.

This love is poured into your hearts. It will not leave you.
Return often to your heart and your memories to visit this love.

Hold your hand out toward the casket.

Extend the blessing of your gratitude as you bid farewell to _____'s physical
presence.

Join hands with one another.

You have the gift of family and friends.
You have the kinship of one another.
You have the presence of God abiding with you.

Although _____'s body will no longer be with you,
his (her) goodness will remain present with you.
All you need to do is place your hand over your heart,
close your eyes, and be still. Let his (her) presence come to you.

You will no longer see his (her) physical face
but you will remember him (her) deep in your soul.
You can carry _____'s goodness with you wherever you are.

Closing Prayer

God of Everlasting Life, _____ is now united with you. Hold tenderly all those who feel sadness and loss at his (her) departure. Risen Christ, ever available to us, sustain each one gathered here. Comfort them as they experience their loss. Draw them to your heart. Assure them that you know their sadness. May they have the strength they need to move through their heartache. Keep hope in their hearts. Amen.

DISTRIBUTION OF CREMAINS

Standing in the Circle of Strength

We begin by standing in a circle, holding hands. We are united in our sorrow and in our love. We remember those who are not here who also treasured _____. This kinship strengthens us. We join with the Holy One who holds us close with compassionate care.

Prayer

Creator of life, we have come to return to earth the physical remains of _____. You lovingly shared her (him) with us. During those years we cherished her (his) presence, imbibed her (his) goodness, and grew strong in her (his) love. All too soon she (he) departed from us. We stand here now in the reality of death. We come to give back the preciousness of this body. It is time to let go, to allow this part of the person we knew to become one with all that is. May the Spirit who breathed on the waters in the beginning of life and who breathed life into her (his) mother's womb, receive the earthen treasure whom we experienced as a beloved presence in our life.

Litany of Consolation

Source of Solace,
touch our hearts with your comfort.

Divine Compassion,
thank you for loaning our loved one to us for a while.

Abiding Presence,
be near when we feel grief's desolation and loneliness.

Star of Hope,
shine in the dark spaces of our emptiness and sorrow.

Holy Wisdom,
provide guidance when we cannot see our way through the pain.

Enduring Love,
wrap your arms around us when we are overcome with sadness.

Rock of Strength,
assure us of our inner resiliency and our ability to heal from the hurt.

Source of Faith,
refine our sense of a life beyond this one and grant us your peace.

Blessing
(As the cremains are held in readiness for the great letting go.)

May the song of birds welcome you with their joy
and the quiet murmur of streams invite you to enter.

May the tenderness of earth embrace you softly
and the freshness of rain fall upon you with care.

May the freedom of the winds and the clouds
carry you on their breath to beautiful places.

May the ocean waves claim you as their companion,
and the stars from whose dust you were formed
smile on you in your return to your ancient home.

Prayer after Distribution

Compassionate One, you surround us with your love. Keep each one here from being overwhelmed by their loss and grief. May they have confidence in your abiding care. Give them strength in the days to come. Amen.

FOR ONE WHO GRIEVES

A small bowl is held in the cradled hands of the one who is grieving.

Cradle the bowl in your hands.

A bowl is meant to hold something.
Let this bowl receive your tears.
They can help you grieve your loss.
Give yourself permission to do so.

Notice the openness of this bowl.
Allow your heart to collect and receive
the treasured memories of your loved one.
May these memories comfort you.

Let the empty bowl's unfilled space
be a symbol of the vacant place in you,
the hollowness created by absence.
Be gentle with yourself.

This bowl was formed and designed
from elements that gave up their original shape.
As you gradually let go of what you once had
may you accept the new form of your life.
Ease into the future with hope.

It took time to create this bowl.
So, too, with your heartache.
The lonely space of loss needs time
before happiness visits your heart.
Be patient with your grief.

Feel how your hands protect
and surround the bowl you hold.
This is how you are cradled
in the loving compassion of God.
Place your trust in this sheltering love.
You are not alone.

In a Time of Grief

Even though I walk through the darkest valley,
I fear no evil; for you are with me;
your rod and your staff—they comfort me.
—Psalm 23:4

Loss clutches my joy and tosses it aside carelessly.
Emptiness follows like a stalker, draining my body of energy.
Confusion interrupts the static flow of my thoughts.
Heartache taunts with a false belief of endless unhappiness.

I turn to you, Friend of those who faced farewells,
for you know the pain of an uninvited goodbye,
you whose mother stood beneath your cross of death,
you who wept at the graveside of a precious friend,
you who gathered your loved ones for a last meal.
Yes, you surely know the hollow chamber of sorrow.

Remind me often that the grief I now experience
comes as the natural consequence of leave-taking.
Ease my impatience when I want to feel better quickly.
Soften any anger, bitterness, or disappointment.
Free me of fears and worries regarding the future.
Bind my heart to you through the kindness of people
whose caring presence remains steadfast while I mourn.

Assure me each day and night that I am not alone—
you are with me, a comforting presence in this dark valley.

Tree Memorial in Honor of the Deceased

Trees are the earth's endless efforts
to speak to the listening heavens.
—Rabindranath Tagore

The breath of creation surrounds this place. The growing things of earth, the creatures, the wind and sun, join us in honoring _____, whose life added so much to the richness of our existence. Let us pause and receive the beauty and refreshment of this place as we remember the presence of this dear one in our lives.

Blessing

May each person who pauses by the beauty of this memorial be touched by the loving spirit of _____.

May all who come here with grief to be tended or old wounds to be mended, find an easing of their sorrows and struggles.

May those whose hearts sing of joy find their happiness deepened and enhanced by this special place. May the laughter of _____ echo in the hearts of each one who visits here.

May anyone carrying an inner burden of any type, discover a peace that eases anxiety and distress. May the quietness of this memorial soften what is difficult for them.

As this tree grows taller and wider, may those who stop here find their faith likewise growing stronger, and the love in their hearts reaching further.

Together: _____, we know you have not left us completely. Your spirit is present here in ways we have yet to discover. Thank you for what you added to our lives when you lived among us. We cherish your memory and will hear your whispers in the wind, your love in the warmth of the sunshine, and your gladness resounding in the birdsongs. The beauty and tranquility of this place assures us that all shall be well.

To close, join hands and pray the Our Father (or other familiar prayer).

Lent

Body Blessing for Lent

This blessing is meant to be led by the presider of the Ash Wednesday liturgy or a Lenten prayer service. The presider invites those present to stand in pairs, facing one another. Those being blessed remain silent. The presider speaks the blessing while those facing each other place their hands next to the part of the other person's body that is being blessed. The final three lines that the presider speaks are repeated to each other by those being blessed.

Forehead

May the Gospel teachings about non-judgment resound in your thoughts of others.

Ears

May you listen closely to how God invites you to grow spiritually during this Lenten season.

Eyes

May you slow down and look more intently in order to find God's movement in your life.

Shoulders

May you carry your cross of difficulties with courage, trusting God's strength to uphold you.

Hands

May your service be so intertwined with God that this love overflows from your heart.

Heart

May you keep turning your heart toward God and allow this love to be reflected in the way you live your life.

Feet

May you welcome God's companionship and guidance as you travel the path of life.

Whisper to the other person:
Return with all your heart.
Remember the Holy Spirit dwells in you.
Be at peace.

Carrying Crosses

Holy One who journeys with me on the road of life with its hills and valleys,

May I recognize the daily cross that is mine and carry this burden in a trustful way, confident that the undesired parts of my life can be guides to my spiritual growth.

Teach me how to be with my personality traits that I consider unworthy or unacceptable.

Inspire me to release my tight grip when I wrestle with the resistant part of myself, the one that insists on having everything in life turn out the way I desire or demand.

Increase my awareness of the false judgments, the unfair expectations that quickly arise to crowd out kindness and compassion for myself and others.

Lessen unrestrained fears and tedious worries that keep me imprisoned in turmoil and confusion, thus diminishing my spirit's strength and ability to reach beyond myself.

Soften any hardness of heart I have toward another. Increase my ability to be understanding. Help me topple the walls that prevent my being a forgiving person.

Expand my perception of the good things my life already holds. Decrease apprehension about not having enough, being enough, doing enough, or growing enough.

Awaken the undying song of hope in my soul as I carry my unwanted cross each day, so that even in the worst of times I continue to trust you to provide what is needed.

Confident of your grace and daily empowerment, I give myself to you as fully as I am able at this time. As I carry the crosses that are mine, remind me often that you are always with me and never against me. I place my desire for union with you into your loving care. Amen.

A LENTEN PRAYER

~

"Why do you see the speck in your neighbor's eye
but do not notice the log in your own eye?
Or how can you say to your neighbor,
'Friend, let me take out the speck in your eye,'
when you yourself do not see the log
in your own eye?"

—Luke 6:42

Holy One, you created me in my mother's womb.
You know the core goodness residing within me.
You also know my propensity for self-orientation.
You see how I want others to grow and change.
You know the thoughts and feelings that run rampant
when I encounter someone whose behavior I dislike.

If I say, "Surely I can get this person to be as I want,"
nudge me insistently with your grace-filled message:
"Leave the other person's transformation alone.
Tend to your own aspects that need to be altered."

In this Lenten season, guide me to a clearer awareness.
Lead me to move beyond a wish to transform others.
Focus my attention on the personal renewal I resist.
May I become more alert and accepting of the reality
that the only person I can set about changing is myself.

Moving Out of Exile

~

By the rivers of Babylon
there we sat down and there we wept
when we remembered Zion.
How could we sing the Lord's song
in a foreign land?
—Psalm 137:1, 4

1. We are moving away from what holds us in bondage, choosing to depart from that which keeps us unfree and unable to access the best of our true self.
2. We are traveling out of "the foreign land" that claims our energy and vitality, leaving the pressure to live according to others' burdensome expectations.
3. We are coming home to that place within us that longs for our acceptance and understanding, coming into the embrace of our own nurturance and compassion.
4. We are saying farewell to the land of old messages and buried emotions that have detained us, leaving behind a history that no longer holds power over us.
5. We are turning toward our inner beauty and goodness, led by the God of Exiles to discover more of the hidden treasures that long to be called home.
6. We are reclaiming what cries out for recognition and ownership, taking back the part of us lost during our sojourn of separation from our peacefulness.
7. We are extending a confident hand toward the slow-to-trust part of our self, befriending it and calling on our courage to find its way back into our life.
8. We are remembering possibilities for growth, the promise of transformation that comes when we no longer ignore our ability to love unreservedly.
9. We are moving from our experience of disengagement, heading toward community, willing to support others who search for what is missing in their lives.
10. We are entering ever more fully into relationship with the Divine. Whenever we are in exile, this Compassionate One travels with us, companioning us until we find the road that sings the song toward home.

OPENING THE HEART TO LOVE

Namasté. The Love in me greets the Love in you.

Reading: from *A Return to Love*, Marianne Williamson

Love is energy. It's not something we can perceive with our physical senses, but people can usually tell you when they feel it and when they don't. Very few people feel enough love in their lives because the world has become a rather loveless place. We can hardly imagine a world in which all of us were in love, all the time, with everyone. There would be no more wars because we wouldn't fight. There would be no hunger because we would feed each other. There would be no environmental breakdown because we would love ourselves, our children and our planet too much to destroy it. There would be no prejudice, oppression or violence of any kind. There would be no sorrow. There would only be peace. . . . We need love in order to live happily, as much as we need oxygen in order to live at all.

Meditation (Based on 1 Corinthians 13:4–8)

In the quiet repose of your mind and heart, repeat each of the following statements to yourself. Pause after each statement. Repeat it five times. Then move on to the next statement.

Love is patient.
Love is kind.
Love is not envious or boastful or arrogant or rude.
Love does not insist on its own way.
Love is not irritable or resentful.
Love does not rejoice in wrongdoing.
Love rejoices in the truth.
Love bears all things.
Love never ends.

Prayer

Open our hearts to you, Source of All Souls,
you whose love dwells within and among us.

Open us to believe how fully we are welcomed by you
each moment of our lives.

Open us to carry our union with you
to those who are a part of our daily encounters.

Open us when we are weary, when we resist,
when we forget, when we doubt, when we are anxious.

Open our hearts to full confidence,
to the trust that we have more than enough love to give away.

Open, open, open us to the journey of love that is ours.

Song

"Love Beyond All Telling," *The Song and the Silence*, Marty Haugen.

THE HOME OF TRANSFORMATION

Prayer is not just spending time with God. It is partly that—but if it ends there, it is fruitless. No, prayer is dynamic. Authentic prayer changes us—unmasks us, strips us, indicates where growth is needed. Authentic prayer never leads us to complacency, but needles us, makes us uneasy at times. It leads us to true self-knowledge, to true humility.

—St. Teresa of Avila

When the heart slowly sinks
into the mire of unhappiness,
when the mind insistently whispers
about could, must, should and ought,
when the voice of the less-than-whole self
grows irritable and impatient
with the way people are, or are not,
and with the way I am, or am not,
let it all be. Move away. Step aside.
Go to the inner dwelling place
where the Christ-light flames endlessly.
Stand in the center of that Love,
untouched by ego-demands, societal failures,
shattered hopes and unfulfilled yearnings.

Walk past all that hinders kindheartedness
from glowing steadily in my daily routines.
Move into the home of transformation,
into that grace-filled, spacious vessel.
Be restored, repaired, renewed, regenerated.
Come forth with germinating hope, start again
with less control, fewer anticipations,
and more peaceful receptivity
in the container of mind and heart.

Welcome the weak, the hardened, the haughty,
the wounded, the burdened, the pained;
for each and every one of these persons
bears the reflection of my shadowed self,
my own glimpse of what is yet to be purified
in the golden sphere of Christ's love.

Marriage

Anniversary Blessing

A large bowl is placed on a table or altar.

May the bowl's empty space remind you
of the abundant love you have yet to share,
of how much there is still to learn, to enjoy,
and to cherish in the gift of one another.

May the bowl's openness keep you loving
when you wrestle with your differences
and would rather close off and turn away.
May you keep your hearts open to each other.

May the bowl's ability to contain nourishment
nudge you to enrich your relationship
with kindness, patience, understanding,
and ample amounts of forgiveness.

May the sturdiness of the bowl
reflect the enduring faithfulness
that strengthens your marital love
and holds your union together.

May the roundness of the bowl's rim
sharpen your awareness and gratitude
for the circle of family and friends
who support you in both easy and hard times.

May the bowl's capacity for receiving
encourage you to welcome Divine Love,
the Gift that sustains your marriage vows
and deepens your dedication to one another.

GOLDEN WEDDING ANNIVERSARY BLESSING

Lift up your hands to the holy place,
and bless the Lord.
—Psalm 134:2

See I have inscribed you on the
palms of my hands.
—Isaiah 49:16

The Blessing

_____, today we use the symbol of hands as a way to offer a blessing for your fifty years of faithfulness to one another in marriage. When each of you placed your wedding ring on the hand of the other, you said yes to a life of unknowns. You said yes with trust in one another's love and trust in the Holy One to guide you through the years ahead. And here you are, fifty years later, a loving couple who has made it through the uncertainties, the many hills and valleys of life. Your love, united with the Holy One's, protected and refined your commitment to one another.

We join now to pray a blessing of gratitude for you today. Please face each other and join hands. Those present, please extend your hands toward _____ and_____ as we bless them:

We give thanks for your hands that join in friendship and companionship.
We give thanks for your hands that caress one another with tenderness.
We give thanks for your hands that cared for one another when you were ill.
We give thanks for your hands that embrace your children and grandchildren.
We give thanks for the generous help your hands give to one another.
We give thanks for your hands that come together in prayer and worship.
We give thanks for the steadfast work your hands accomplished through the years.
We give thanks for your hands that reach out to welcome others into your home.

*M*ay you go forward this day with gratitude, knowing your kindness and endless efforts have enriched and helped those in your life. Each time you look at your hands may you remember the fifty years of love you offered to each other. As you continue to hold hands, may your faithful love strengthen you in your aging. Remember always that God's love abides in you. Amen.

Marriage Blessing

~

Introduction: from *A Hidden Wholeness*, Parker Palmer

Read by the presider or lector:
There was a time when farmers on the Great Plains, at the first sign of a blizzard, would run a rope from the back door out to the barn. They all knew stories of people who had wandered off and been frozen to death, having lost sight of home in a whiteout while still in their own backyards.

Blessing

The presider wraps a colorful, thick ribbon around the couples' joined hands.

(*Names of the two being married*) _____ and _____, today you enter a journey of life together, a life that finds its source in divine love, enfleshed in your love for one another. Just as ranchers and farmers use a rope to help them find their way in a blinding snowstorm, you will sometimes need to have a strong ribbon of love to help you to find your way back home to the affection you now have for one another. For life is such that you can lose your way to this love in the countless turns and stumbles that will undoubtedly happen in the years to come. With this in mind, I extend the following blessing to you:

May the ribbon of love be the way home to faithfulness when you are tempted to stray.
May the ribbon of love be the way home to joy when you are most in need of it.
May the ribbon of love be the way home to recognition when you fail to see each other's gifts.
May the ribbon of love be the way home to forgiveness when you hurt each other.
May the ribbon of love be the way home to hope when you feel disheartened.
May the ribbon of love be the way home to understanding when differences arise.

May the ribbon of love be the way home to laughter when you yearn for happiness.

May the ribbon of love be the way home to trust when you doubt the other's actions.

May the ribbon of love be the way home to patience when you encounter life's challenges.

May the ribbon of love be the way home to leisure when you are overwhelmed with work.

May the ribbon of love be the way home to God when you are searching for peace.

God of love, _____ and _____ profess their committed love for one another. May they keep you as the center of this love. Please lead them back to the ribbon of love each time they have need of it. Amen.

WEDDING BASKET

⌒

The leader holds a woven basket of several colors. All present respond to each blessing.

This woven basket serves as a metaphor for your marriage. Like the basket, you bring together two personal histories, two ancestries, two stories of life. May your personal narratives provide strength as they weave together in your marriage.

All: **May God's love weave through your lives.**

This basket has a firm, solid base joining each of the sides. Without this sturdy foundation, the rest of the basket would not hold together. May divine love be the strong foundation that gives your marriage strength and endurance.

May God's love weave through your lives.

If you look closely, you can see small flaws among the weaving. As you continue on your journey with one another, the little imperfections of your personalities will reveal themselves. As you discover these, may the blessing of unconditional love and steady patience enable you to welcome and accept each other with continual kindness.

May God's love weave through your lives.

In order for this basket to be woven together, the materials had to be pliable enough to bend, flexible enough to weave without breaking. You each come here with beliefs and values gleaned from your years of living. May you be open and willing to bend your ideas and inclinations when differences arise.

May God's love weave through your lives.

This basket has handles so that it can be easily carried. May your marital relationship be handled with the ease of each other's understanding, forgiveness, and the durable quality of your daily faithfulness.

May God's love weave through your lives.

The weaving together of these grasses forms an open container. This spacious interior symbolizes the abundant love contained in your marriage. May it overflow with joy, and bring you deep happiness and ongoing peace of mind and heart.

May God's love weave through your lives.

May the blessing of the divine Basket Weaver sustain you in your fidelity.
May the Holy One continually weave through your love for one another.
May this love spill over from the basket of your lives and touch those you encounter.
We ask this blessing in the name of the One who holds us all together in love.

Mary

Blessed Encounter

Mary of Nazareth and her beloved cousin Elizabeth,
Each woman with a sacred story secreted in the heart,
Life stirring, quietly nurtured inside a darkened womb.
Each woman living her days with cloudy mystery,
Trusting there will be light enough to follow the way.

What uncertainty gathers daily at their awakening:
How could it be, this growing child each one carries?
Who will this unknown, hidden one in the womb become?
Where will the women, young and old, seek their courage?

Go, Mary, go. Travel to your beloved cousin's doorstep.
Listen, Elizabeth, listen. Someone dear comes down the road.
Open the door and welcome wide this wondrous visitor.
Gasp in amazement at the dance skipping in your womb.

Oh, blessed are you among women, blessed are you.

LITANY OF MARY

Mary of the Annunciation,
teach us how to respond with faith to divine mystery.

Mary at Elizabeth's door,
teach us to be generous with our capacity to care.

Mary giving birth to Jesus,
teach us to look for your Son in our adverse conditions.

Mary fleeing into the strange land of Egypt,
teach us to welcome strangers from foreign lands.

Mary at the Presentation of Jesus,
teach us how to accept the conditions for loving fully.

Mary in the Temple where young Jesus preached,
teach us to be diligent in finding our spiritual treasure.

Mary at home in Nazareth with your family,
teach us to value the gift of our relationships.

Mary at the wedding feast of Cana,
teach us how to humbly ask for what is needed.

Mary meeting Jesus on the way to Calvary,
teach us to meet our own pain with compassion.

Mary standing beneath the Cross,
teach us to be present to the suffering ones of our world.

Mary receiving your crucified Son in your arms,
teach us that we, too, can embrace our losses with courage.

Mary at the tomb,
teach us to be not be afraid to enter into our grief.

Mary in the Upper Room with the disciples,
teach us the strength of community and the power of prayer.

*M*ary, mother of Jesus, we look to your life of faith and draw inspiration from you. The witness of your life readies us to be people of immeasurable love, to give of ourselves wholeheartedly to a life of ongoing transformation. How grateful we are to have you as an exemplar of how to strengthen faith and deepen union with the Holy One.

OPENING OUR SPIRITS AS MARY DID

Then Mary said, "Here I am, the servant of the Lord:
let it be with me according to your word."
—Luke 1:38

Remember Mary's yes to God's request to bear divinity within her.
Hear her response: "Be it done to me according to your word."
Mary was an open vessel. She heard the surprising request made to her.
She struggled with uncertainty. She questioned. Listened. Responded with yes.

Mary was receptive to the incredible mystery of divine love.

We, too, are offered this gift, as Mary was.
We are invited to be open to receive the Christ, not physically, but spiritually.

Imagine your spirit is like the inner space of a beautiful golden bowl.
Look inside the space of that bowl.
See if it contains items that are to be given away.
What gifts might you be holding that could be shared?
Peace? Kindheartedness? Understanding? Tolerance? Charity? Friendliness?

Look into your inner space again.
What sort of unnecessary things are there?
What is taking up space that needs to be discarded in order to welcome Christ?
Hard feelings toward someone? Self-absorption? Envy? Superiority?
Over-attachment?
Toss out anything that might be keeping the golden bowl from being filled
with love.

See how spacious your inner self is, how much room there is for filling.
Take a deep breath and breathe in the goodness of the Holy One.
Fill your golden bowl with the beauty, richness, and power of Christ's love.

Offer thanks to the Holy One for this beautiful love that is ready to fill the
vessel of your deep self.

The Visitation

Namasté. I welcome you into my heart.

Reading 1: Luke 1:39–45, 56

In those days Mary set out and went with haste to a Judean town in the hill country where she entered the house of Zechariah and greeted Elizabeth. When Elizabeth heard Mary's greeting, the child leaped in her womb. And Elizabeth was filled with the Holy Spirit and exclaimed with a loud voice, "Blessed are you among women, and blessed is the fruit of your womb. And why has this happened to me, that the mother of my Lord comes to me? For as soon as I heard the sound of your greeting, the child in my womb leaped for joy. And blessed is she who believed that there would be a fulfillment of what was spoken to her by the Lord. . . ." And Mary remained with her about three months and then returned to her home.

Response

Hail Mary, full of grace, the Holy One is with you.
Blessed are you among women, and blessed is the fruit of your womb, Jesus.

Reading 2: from *Enter the Story*, Fran Ferder

The flow of events is simple but potent: Mary goes with haste. She enters the house. She greets Elizabeth. Elizabeth hears Mary. The child in Elizabeth's womb "leaps." Elizabeth is filled with a sense of the holy. She proclaims a blessing upon Mary. Mary responds.

Entering. Greeting. Hearing. Feeling. Blessing. Responding. The simple visit of these two women offers us a vivid example of the structure of healthy/ holy human encounter. It gives us a glimpse of what can unfold when we meet one another on the inside. Though words are few, and details of this biblical visitation are spare, when Mary takes her leave, both women are more aware of who they are, before one another and before God. They have claimed their voices and been heard. They are blessed. That is what true meeting ought to effect in us each time we come together.

Meditation

The Old One (the Wise One) in us is greeted by the Young One who is pregnant with some aspect of Christ waiting to come alive in us. Go to the place in you where your Wise One resides. Find her peace and goodness, her compassion and hospitality. Rest there awhile.

Then let the Young One greet the Old One in yourself. Receive the Young One's passion for life, her trust and enthusiasm, her confidence in what is yet to come.

Now have the Old One in you welcome this Young One, invite her into your life—the part of you that is still unknown and unbirthed, the part of you waiting to come alive.

- Be with the generosity of welcome.
- Be with the hiddenness of what is yet to be.
- Be with the unconditional love of the Old One.
- Be with the faith and trust of the Young One.
- Surrender any concern, doubt, skepticism, fear.
- Open to what is now firmly at home in yourself.
- Open to what is yet to be known and welcomed.

Pause to recall the people in your life who have greeted you in a way that welcomed you wholeheartedly, believed in you, and assured you of the goodness, the God-ness, within you. Call their names out as a way of honoring these persons.

Closing

"The Song of Mary" (Luke 1:46–55)

Meditations

CRADLED BY THE DIVINE MOTHER

Settle into a comfortable posture (sitting or lying down).
Take time to let your mind and body slow down and become quiet.
You might do this by noticing the steady rhythm of your heartbeat.

Call upon the Divine Mother to be with you.
Her sacred presence holds the essence of wisdom.
Visualize this divine being filled with radiant light,
a calming luminosity glowing around her.

Imagine that you are a young child, two or three years old.
The Divine Mother opens her arms with a wide welcome
ready to receive you with a heartfelt embrace.
Place your trust in this loving presence.
Go to the Divine Mother with complete confidence.

She lifts you carefully onto her spacious lap,
holds you with tender compassion and kindness.
You receive the most incredible, cradling love.
Let this love move through your entire being,
bringing with it a deep, relaxing peace.

As you are cradled by this eternal mothering love,
you hear the Divine Mother humming softly to you.
Her lullaby enters every pore of your being.
Be still and let yourself be cradled by this comforting love.

Surrender to the stillness. Become one with the Divine Mother.
Gradually, there is no separation between the two of you.
You merge with her harmonious light and love.
You want for nothing. You have all that you need.

Remain in this state of oneness for as long as possible.
Carry the light-filled presence of the Divine Mother within you
as you leave your place of meditation.

Dwell

~

Dwell as near as possible
to the channel
in which your life flows.
—Henry David Thoreau

Dwell . . .

Be at home with the deeper part of yourself. Slow your hurry in order to focus on what truly matters. Ask yourself each day what you need in order to stay near this vital center. Inhabit the dimensions of your life in such a way that an abiding peace flows quietly in you.

as near as possible . . .

No need to be a perfectionist about the desire to be close to what counts most to you. Set forth reasonable expectations. Be kind to yourself when you lose touch with this essential aspect. Give yourself to your central focus repeatedly. Take courage. Have hope. Trust what matters most.

to the channel . . .

Identify the current out of which your beliefs and values flow. What core intention moves your thoughts, feelings, actions? Is it to be a channel of the Holy One's love? Perhaps it is a yearning to change an attitude or a way of living? Only you know.

in which your life . . .

Your life. Not someone else's. Pull back from comparisons and envies. Be patient and lovingly honest with how you maintain this most important center of your inner world. Acknowledge your desire to be faithful. Seek kinship and support to help you be true.

flows . . .

Notice what throws you off course or distracts you from being with what your heart deems worthy. Be willing to part ways with whatever keeps the deep waters of your soul from moving freely, lovingly, peacefully.

Dwell as near as possible to the channel in which your life flows.

QUIETING BODY AND SPIRIT

Let your body become still.
Picture yourself in a warm, soothing bubble bath or a refreshing shower.
It is warm, comforting, relaxing.
Feel the calming, restful bliss of the water against your skin.
Let it wash over you and rinse away any pain or stress.
Notice a sense of well-being moving from your head to your toes.
Let out a deep sigh. Release anything that keeps your body tense.
Rest in the quieting waters.

Let your mind become still.
Picture a smooth, tranquil lake without a ripple on the clear water.
The quiet lake contains a perfect reflection of trees and blue sky.
Let go of all troublesome thoughts and worrisome concerns.
Allow only this scene of serenity to suffuse your mental image.
Look again at the lake's stillness.
Allow its calmness and clearness to hush your thoughts.
Your mind is peaceful, relaxed, at ease.

Let your emotions become still.
Imagine you hear a silver bell ring with one clear gong.
The sound has a soft, resonant tone.
Hear the silver bell ring again.
The vibration feels delicate, yet strong, as it moves through you.
Let the sound of the bell soothe anything that holds discord.
You begin to relax. Your feelings grow calm, harmonious.
Hear the silver bell ring one more time.
All within you becomes quiet and at peace.

Let your spirit become still.
Imagine that you are in a flourishing garden.
The sunshine, butterflies, and birds welcome you.
As you walk along, you sense that you are not alone.
No one can be seen. Not a word is spoken.
Yet you know a gracious Presence is with you.
You have a profound sense of being loved.

Breathe in this love. Savor your happiness.
Dwell freely and fully in this exquisite kindness.
Be at peace.

RITUAL OF FORGIVENESS

A stone that fits into the palm of your hand will be used for this ritual.

1. Read the passage of the woman caught in adultery (Jn 8:1–11).
    What must it have felt like to be the woman accused?
    (to be rejected, judged, threatened, treated harshly, and hurt by others)
    What was it like to be the accusers?
    (to feel self-righteous anger about the law being broken, to want to hurl suffering and pain at another)

2. Hold a good-sized stone in your right hand.
    Think about how others have thrown stones at you, how you have been hurt.
    Has someone in particular threatened, hurt, or rejected you?
    Recall the specific suffering you've known because of the stones of others.
    Consider this to be the stone of your suffering.
    Notice how this stone feels in your hand.

3. Now, hold the stone in your left hand.
    Think about those persons at whom you have thrown stones.
    How have you hurt others? Recall a specific instance.
    Is there anyone in your life at whom you currently want to aim a stone?
    Consider this to be the stone of others' suffering.
    Notice how this stone feels in your hand.

4. Go back to the story of the woman caught in adultery.
    Visualize Jesus coming to her, looking upon her with mercy.
    See the forgiving love he extends to her.
    Now visualize Jesus looking upon you with this same merciful love.
    Then see him look with this same love upon those you want to stone.

5. Hold the stone between your hands, one hand on the bottom, the other on the top.
    Feel the warmth that comes from your hands onto the stone.
    Imagine the forgiveness of the Holy One being a warmth around your heart.

Pray to be healed of the hurts in your life.

Ask for a desire and an intention to forgive those who have hurt you.

Pray for those you have knowingly hurt in some way.

Ask for remorse and the hope of being forgiven by those you have harmed.

6. When you are ready, go and put your stone at the foot of a cross, or out in a garden, by a river, lake, or under a tree. Do this as a sign of your intention to let go of the hurts you bear, and to receive forgiveness for the hurts you have caused.

As you do this, pray these adapted lines from the Our Father:

"Forgive me for the hurts I've caused as I forgive those who have hurt me."

It may take some time of holding the stone before you are ready and able to let go of the stone. Keep bringing this intention to your prayer. Be patient with however long you need.

Seeking Healing

Reading: Luke 8:40–48

As he went, the crowds pressed in on him. Now there was a woman who had been suffering from hemorrhages for twelve years; and though she had spent all she had on physicians, no one could cure her. She came up behind him and touched the fringe of his clothes, and immediately her hemorrhage stopped. Then Jesus asked, "Who touched me?" When all denied it, Peter said, "Master, the crowds surround you and press in on you." But Jesus said, "Someone touched me; for I noticed that power had gone out from me." When the woman saw that she could not remain hidden, she came trembling; and falling down before him, she declared in the presence of all the people why she had touched him, and how she had been immediately healed. He said to her, "Daughter, your faith has made you well; go in peace."

Meditation

Imagine the scene, the crowd gathered around Jesus. A woman named Sabina stands at a distance, sees and hears Jesus speaking in front of the people, who listen intently. She doesn't feel well. She never feels well. She is continually weak from loss of blood. She is so tired of being ill. Added to that, Sabina feels great fear, knowing she ought not be there. Jewish law states that if she is menstruating, she contaminates the people she touches.

Sabina slowly walks up to the crowd, at first, standing by the edge of it. Then she senses inside of her an insatiable need to be closer; if she can just be next to the Healer, she will have a chance to be well. She struggles with her fear and her indecision whether to leave or to take the risk of staying and possibly being healed. Her long years of bleeding lead Sabina to make a dangerous choice. How wonderful it would be to feel well again. She will take the risk. She cares about herself enough to go ahead and move closer.

Then Sabina takes a deep breath, slowly nudges her way between the people who are standing tightly together. With every step she knows she is breaking the law, that she could be stoned for what she is doing. But her desire to care for herself grows gradually stronger than her fear.

Finally she is just one row away from Jesus. Oh, how amazing his voice, how caring he sounds. She doesn't want to be noticed so she crouches down to a low posture, praying her presence will not be detected. Oh, how she longs to be well.

Then, with a sudden burst of courage she reaches out to Jesus, hoping to simply touch him. That will be enough. Sabina's fingers feel the texture of cloth. She has actually touched the hem of his robe! At this moment, a strong current of energy rushes through her. This is like nothing she has ever felt before. Joy and astonishment vibrate in her body and spirit. She feels new, fresh, released.

In that moment Sabina knows without a doubt she no longer bleeds. She feels a tug on the robe as it slips from her hand. Jesus turns. Trepidation rises up in her. What if she has been discovered? Then she hears him ask: "Who is it that touched me? I felt power go out from me."

The people look around and then someone looks down at her. Sabina can no longer hide. She must stand and claim her healing. She responds, "I am the one who touched you." As she speaks these words, Jesus smiles at her, reaches out, takes the healed woman's hands and helps her to stand up. Sabina beams with happiness and Jesus assures her that she has been restored to good health.

Now put yourself in the place of this brave and faith-filled woman. What part of your life has troubled you or caused you distress for a long time? Maybe it's something about your own personality or spiritual life, or a painful aspect of a relationship that continually fails to be what you long for it to be. Perhaps it is a chronic illness, or a dream for something that still has not come into reality.

When you have named this part of your life, take it to Jesus. Entrust yourself and your need to him. He looks on you with an easy acceptance. See the welcome on his face, receive the flow of kindness, the power and strength of compassion that come to you from this great Healer.

Open your whole being and receive this restorative love. Allow it to flood your mind and heart, your own being. Let it be a current of peace that glides from your head down to your toes.

Sit in stillness with this healing presence for as long as you wish.

THE CONTAINER OF YOUR HEART

Hold a small bowl in your hands or bring your hands together in the shape
of one.

 Notice the openness in your hands. The readiness of the space to be filled.
 The container of your hands represents the container of your heart.
 Reflect on each of the following aspects of a bowl in relation to your heart.

Blessing Bowl: gratitude for parts of your life that are fruitful and abundant
  Let it be a symbol of abundance.
  Gather your many blessings and
  visualize them filling the bowl.
  Offer thanks to the One who gifts.

Beggar's Bowl: where you lack energy, vitality; where you feel empty or wanting
  Let it be your beggars bowl.
  Hold it out silently, with trust,
  believing that what you need
  will be given to you by the Holy One.

Bowl of Dreams: what longs to come to life in you
  Let it contain your dreams.
  Place within it your inmost hopes.
  Unite in love with the Divine Dreamer,
  the One who fills your spirit with a passion for life.

Bowl of Suffering: what wants to be relieved and healed
  Place within it your own hurts and difficulties.
  Remember others needing a release from suffering.
  Bring into your bowl those from far and near
  who can benefit from your compassionate love.

Bowl of Spiritual Kinship: your connection with others
  Remember those who have assisted your inner growth,
  Those who nurtured and enriched you spiritually.
  Fill your bowl with gratitude for them.
  Thank the Holy One for the blessing of kinship.

Set down the bowl and place your hands over your heart. Breathe a full, strong breath. Sense it circulating through your body. Remember that your heart is a container of Divine Love. Receive the strength and courage this Love brings. Be in quiet union with the gift of divine resilience within you.

YOU ARE GOD'S TEMPLE

Do you not know that you are God's temple
and that God's spirit dwells in you?
—1 Corinthians 3:16

Meditation

Imagine that you have within you a magnificent cathedral.
Inside this cathedral there are tall, stained glass windows,
a vast ceiling, and finely polished wood on the floors.
Bright sunlight streams through the windows,
infusing the atmosphere with a gentle peacefulness.

Imagine that this cathedral is the center of your heart.
In the middle of your cathedral is an immense Love.
This Love believes in you,
cares about you,
longs for you intensely.
This Love sees only good in you.
This Loves cherishes you and continually offers you a place of rest.

You are surrounded and imbued with this Love.
As you feel the beat of your heart, unite with this immense Love.
As you breathe in, breathe in peace.
As you breathe out, let yourself be filled with stillness.

Dwell in this place of unconditional love and sweet harmony.
Let yourself just be in the presence of this abiding kindness.

Prayer

O Divine Spirit resting within me,
how precious is your presence.
I am your temple, your cathedral.
How humbling that I could be

the abode of your unconditional love.
May the dwelling I provide for you
be one of ceaseless contemplation.
Shine in the window of my soul
and keep my heart swept clean.
O Divine Spirit resting within me,
all is yours now, all is yours.

Ministry

A Listening Heart

For those who accompany another as a spiritual guide.
Namasté. I greet the listening heart in you.

Reading 1: from *Holy Listening*, Margaret Guenther

Domination and submission are not what spiritual direction is about, but "holy listening," presence and attentiveness. . . . The spiritual director may be tempted to fix things . . . To combat such temptation, it is good to remember the spiritual maxim offered by John Irving in one of his novels: when you help people, you mess with them. . . . The director has agreed to put herself aside so that her total attention can be focused on the other person sitting in the other chair. What a gift to bring to another, the gift of disinterested, loving attention!

Reading 2: from *Finding What You Didn't Lose*, John Fox

When someone deeply listens to you
it is like holding out a dented cup
you've had since childhood
and watching it fill up with
cold, fresh water.
When it balances on top of the brim,
you are understood.
When it overflows and touches your skin
you are loved.

When someone deeply listens to you,
the room where you stay
starts a new life
and the place where you wrote
your first poem
begins to flow in your mind's eye.
It is as if gold has been discovered!

When someone deeply listens to you,
your bare feet are on the earth

and a beloved land that seemed distant
is now at home within you.

Litany of Affirmations
(for the one who companions another)

You will set aside your own story to listen fully to another's.
You will hear revelations that evoke tears in your heart.
You will listen to joys that make you want to cheer.
You will be silent when speech would only get in the way.
You will witness amazing strength in those who have suffered.
You will speak with the wisdom of the One who breathes in you.
You will draw strength from knowing you are not in charge.
You will watch how growth happens in surprising ways.
You will wait patiently while deep healing takes place.
You will be aware of your ego when it wants to take over.
You will be inspired by seeing how the Divine moves in another.
You will offer compassion to those who find life difficult.
You will affirm those who choose fresh ways to inner peace.
You will be grateful for the privilege and gift of companioning others.

*L*istener of our Deepest Self, the ear of your heart is forever attentive to us. We call and you respond. We turn and you embrace. We look and you gaze. We search and you lead. We lose and you find. We wander and you return us home. Grant us the grace to be a reflection of your presence. Remind us often to let go of vain ambition when it pushes us to control or impede what you are stirring within the one whom we companion. Thank you for the privilege of walking with those who desire to set their hearts on you. Amen.

Blessing of a Church Minister

~

The only way by which we unite ourselves to the Divine in us is by
longing with every cell of our body and our mind to be one with
the Beloved. It is the only way. And that longing has to be perpet-
ual, permanent, it has to go on as a river in the heart, a cry in the
heart, saying endlessly: Take me to you, take me to you.
                                        —Andrew Harvey

May you listen to the Holy One in each aspect of your life,
        especially in those places that seem least likely to reveal divinity
May your daily prayer lead you back into your ministry
        with enthusiasm and dedication.
May you recognize the pastoral fruits of your service
        and not be discouraged when they are unclear.
May your practice of compassion be a source of spiritual transformation
        for you and for our world.
May the burdens and difficult things of your ministry
        be eased as you lean on the heart of the Divine Beloved.
May you give generously of your time, energy and talents,
        and graciously receive the assistance others offer to you.
May you walk faith-filled and confident
        through the many adventures of your life and ministry.
May thanksgiving overflow in your heart
        and be frequently proclaimed in your life.
May you be clothed in the calmness of the Life-Giver's peace
        and the strength of the Life-Giver's kindness.
May you long for the Holy One in every cell of your being
        so that you might bear the power of this Love.
_____, may your heart be centered on the Holy One
        who is the ultimate source of spiritual guidance.

In Giving We Receive

All I received, I gave away,
in ever new gifts, in ever new songs.
—Rabindranath Tagore

Introduction

Life swings us between the rhythm of giving and receiving. Too often "giving" maintains a strong hold on us and "receiving" shrinks significantly when we are involved in service. As we renew our intention to enter into our work wholeheartedly, what do we most want to share with others? What do we desire to receive? How willing are we to make decisions that contribute to a balance between these two actions? As we join in prayer, let these questions be uppermost in our mind and heart.

Meditation

Sit with palms open on your lap. Notice the rhythm of giving and receiving that is part of your breathing. Breathing in, you receive life-giving oxygen for the body. Breathing out, you give carbon dioxide to the parts of nature that cannot live without it. The rhythm of our physical breathing is similar to the rhythm of ministry. We breathe in—we receive. We breathe out—we give.

Enter into meditation with the quiet rhythm of the following breath prayer.
Breathing in . . . "I receive. "
Breathing out . . . "I give away."

Reading 1: Luke 6:38

"Give and it will be given to you. A good measure, pressed down, shaken together, running over, will be put into your lap; for the measure you give will be the measure you get back."

Reading 2: 2 Corinthians 9:6–8

The point is this: the one who sows sparingly will also reap sparingly, and the one who sows bountifully will also reap bountifully. Each of you must give as you have made up your mind, not reluctantly or under compulsion, for God loves a cheerful giver. And God is able to provide you with every blessing in abundance so that by always having enough of everything, you may share abundantly in every good work.

Reading 3 from "The Law of Giving," in *Seven Spiritual Laws of Success*, Deepak Chopra

The universe operates through dynamic exchange . . .
giving and receiving are different aspects
of the flow of energy in the universe.
And in our willingness to give that which we seek,
we keep the abundance of the universe circulating in our lives.

Proclamation:
A Time for Giving and a Time for Receiving

There is a time to give and a time to receive:
    a time to breathe in and a time to breathe out.
    a time to wake up and a time to go to sleep.
    a time to speed up and a time to slow down.
    a time to speak and a time to listen.
    a time to be active and a time to be still.
    a time to give gifts and a time to accept them.
    a time to serve and a time to be served.
    a time to pray alone and a time to pray together.
    a time to be strong and a time to be vulnerable.
    a time to hold on and a time to let go.
    a time to read and a time to reflect.
    a time to laugh and a time to be serious.
    a time to reach out and a time to withhold.
    a time to give away and a time to gather back.

a time to extend kindness and a time to receive it.
a time to embrace and a time to be embraced.
All: **A time to love and a time to be loved.**

Quiet Reflection: from "Did I Love Well?" in *A Path with Heart*, Jack Kornfield

To see the preciousness of all things, we must bring our full attention to life. . . . As the qualities of presence and simplicity begin to permeate more and more of our life, our inner love for the earth and all beings begins to express itself and brings our path alive. . . .

Cast your memory back across your whole life and bring to mind two good deeds that you have done, two things that you did that were good. They need not be grandiose; let whatever wants to arise show itself . . . Almost everyone who is able to remember such deeds discovers them to be remarkably simple. They are rarely deeds one would put on a resume. . . .

- Ponder your past experience of service:
- A good deed someone did for you that made a difference.
- A good deed you did for someone else that made a difference.

Commitment to Give/Receive

Response to each: **I give generously. I receive gratefully.**
When I am asked to go the extra mile and then some . . .
When I listen to an endless talker with my full attention . . .
When I open my mind to set aside judgment and bias . . .
When I turn toward a difficult person I prefer to ignore . . .
When I accept another's help even if I can do it myself . . .
When I take a big risk and speak out for justice . . .
When I give of my time rather than keep it for myself . . .
When I allow myself to be vulnerable instead of being strong . . .
When I let others take over rather than demanding to be in charge . . .
When I listen to affirmations about the worth of my ministry . . .

Prayer

*J*esus, we turn to you, our model and mentor of giving and receiving. We recall how you poured yourself out in service to those who crowded around you. We bear in mind, too, how you withdrew to the mountainsides to pray and restore what was depleted in your body and spirit. Grant us, Giver of Gifts, the wisdom, inspiration, and discipline to cultivate a healthy balance between generous service to others and compassionate care of ourselves. Amen.

MINISTRY BLESSING

May you look for Christ's presence within your ministry, especially in those persons and places that seem least likely to reveal this unshakable Love.

May you give generously and patiently of your time, energy, and talents when they are needed, and receive graciously the assistance that others offer to you.

May you set aside the distractions of endless tasks and duties to listen with a generous heart and mind to those who bring their sorrows and joys to you.

May you find a trusted companion who journeys compassionately with you, tending to your spirit as you seek comfort and clarity for your life.

May you be clothed in the calmness of Jesus and the strength of his kindness, so that anxiety and fear do not strangle you in their tenacious grip.

May you recognize the fruits of your ministry and pause to give thanks for this bounty, no matter how small or insignificant these fruits might appear.

May your hope be restored when it weakens with discouragement; may you trust that your efforts at discipleship are worthwhile.

May you be attentive to what rises within you mentally and emotionally, recognizing how this affects your approach to what you do.

May the love that overflows from your heart to others be returned to you a hundredfold from those who receive the blessing of your ministry.

May you walk faith-filled and confident through the emerging undertakings and surprising developments that come your way.

May you return often to the Gospels and find within the life of Jesus and his teachings the inspiration required for dedicated service.

May you remember that your ministry finds its source in the One whose "power working through you can do more than you could ask or imagine" (Eph 3:21).

May your heart continually be centered on the Holy One, remain faithful to daily prayer, and be led back into your ministry with enthusiasm and renewed dedication.

Peace be with you.

SERENADE OF THE SONG SPARROW

Outside my small cabin
hidden among the birch and pines
on a northern Minnesota bluff
a song sparrow opens the dawn
with the first of an all-day
serenade.

Cheerful and clear it awakens
not only my sleepy eyes
but my drowsy heart
dulled with its endless effort
to meet the ego's requirements.

Long into the afternoon
and through the last layers of sunset
this tiny creature sings,
sings, sings, sings
of what I do not know,
perhaps simply for the bliss
of being alive in this lovely land.
A happy song
wrapped in the joy
I often fail to notice
amid my self-created burdens.

When I leave this holy place
will the chirpy cadence of the song sparrow
stay with me?

Will it turn me toward the serenade of joy
that is only a breath away?

UNWANTED TASKS

Doing things we do not want to do,
cleaning a house, going to work,
packing a suitcase, tending a child,
flossing teeth, telling the truth,
preparing a meal, forgiving a hurt,
weeding the garden, buying food.

Each day something gets in the way
of a perfect life, uproots the dream
of everything sailing along exactly
as we planned and desired.

How to live with the dross and
the dreadful, the tasteless tasks,
the unbidden requirements,
the silent requests to be a best self.

How to savor what floats between
the unwanted things: the trickles of
kindness, the sudden entrance of a thought
settling our inner disturbance,
the chance meeting of a blue sky, a kiss
breathing through body and soul,
the unexpected hour of free space
allowing time to unburden a schedule.

Drifters we are, pilgrims, too. And sometimes
exiles fearing we will never get back to
the place inside that cradles us like home.
We let ourselves be imprisoned by what
we do not want, missing the elegant life
sashaying among the undesired duties.

New Year

Barbour's Universe

I walk along the thin lines
of my January calendar,
fractured by speeding Time
that is not Time at all,
only my chalky illusion
marking off the minutes
of quickly flowing years,

but I continue to march dutifully
to the forceful beat of Time
in the Gulag of my mind,
allowing this imagined enemy
to threaten my tranquility.

How is it I allow myself
to be ruled by a strong phantom
not even there?
How is it I force myself
to fit within the frozen parameters
of a non-existent structure?

What weevil of falseness
chewed its deceitful way
into the soft recesses of my brain,
convincing me that Time
can whip me into false obedience?

Based on the theory of Julian Barbour in The End of Time

LETTING GO AND WELCOMING

Each new year extends an invitation to re-enter the process of transformation, for self and for our world. We stand at the threshold, looking back and looking ahead. This valuable process involves *a deliberate letting go of the past* and an *intentional welcoming of future possibilities*. We will make choices and decisions in the coming year that will create our reality. We live on a wounded planet and share life in a world of suffering humanity. But we do not despair. The Holy One continues to awaken us. We have what we need to bring peace within ourselves and our world. This is my prayer for each and all of us.

Pause to reflect on what you might need to let go of from the past year. (An old grudge, a certain attitude or behavior, some strong emotion hindering your spiritual growth, an aspect of self that got out of hand, etc.)

Look toward the new year by asking "What is it I want to welcome?" (A change in approach to self or others, some particular virtue or quality, greater involvement in changing systems of justice, etc.)

> To let go of the idea that I am separate from the rest of creation.
> To welcome the vast opportunities to unite with my surroundings.
>
> To let go of whatever keeps me indifferent to the suffering of others.
> To draw forth and act on the compassion stored within me.
>
> To let go of inattentiveness to beauty dwelling around me.
> To welcome the joys and surprising wonders each day contains.
>
> To let go of past grievances and tightly-held hurts that I carry.
> To welcome and act on my ability to forgive and be healed.
>
> To let go of aversion and avoidance of what is unwanted.
> To welcome people and events that disturb my comfort zone.
>
> To let go of the pull of consumerism on my desires and values.
> To welcome simple living and the plenitude that is mine.
>
> To let go of being imprisoned by stingy self-centeredness.
> To welcome the ways that life lures forth my ability to love.

To let go of what stalls or impedes my spiritual growth.
To welcome quiet times to be with the Keeper of my Heart.

To let go of worry about things over which I have no control.
To welcome a stronger trust in the Holy One that all shall be well.

To let go of the desire to have a perfect, undisturbed life.
To welcome the taken-for-granted peacefulness I already have.

To let go of cherished ones who have departed this sphere of life.
To welcome the steadfast love and good memories they left behind.

To let go of the old year's troubles and unresolved burdens.
To welcome the new year with hope and a sense of adventure.

*H*oly One, from long ago people have sought your light to guide their way. As the new year opens, enable me to be more fully yours. Guide me in letting go of what keeps me from growing. Lead me to know and welcome what will enlarge my love for you. Amen.

New Year Ritual for Women

A large candle, two plates, two small pieces of paper per person, pens or pencils will be used.

Reflection: Statement of Commitment

Consider your dedication, commitment, purpose, or goal for the new year. Write a one sentence statement that describes this. This statement will not be shared. Write your name on the back of the paper. Place the papers on the plate with the name showing. (This plate is then placed by a lit candle in the center of the circle.)

Reflection: Blessings of the New Year

Now take the other piece of paper. Reflect on what you most long for in this new year for each one who is present. Write that one central blessing (a word, phrase, or sentence) on the piece of paper.

Collect all the blessings. Place them with the writing face down on the second plate. Pass the plate around the circle. Each participant takes one paper from the plate and reads aloud the blessing she has received.

Prayer of Remembrance

As we proceed into this new year, we pause and bring to mind women whose presence has enlivened us and cheered us onward:

The women of long ago whose love and goodness reached through the years to our hearts and helped us to be who we are today.

Courageous women whose voice has been strong, who struggled and were vulnerable so we could have the freedoms we easily take for granted, such as the right to vote and the ability to use our talents in the way we choose.

Discerning women who helped us go deeper, to believe in and trust our intuition, who encouraged us to take time for nurturing our inner space.

Women who have inspired us be the best we can be, women who stretched our minds and hearts to reach beyond our securities, who challenged us to grow; women who never gave up on us.

Nurturing women who drew near and cared for us, extended comfort in our hurt and loss; women who were there for us in our time of need.

Women of the gospels, especially Mary of Nazareth and Mary of Magdala; women whose witness of faith, discipleship, and goodness encourages us to be all we can be spiritually.

Each woman here today with her wisdom and her grace; each one who listens to that wisdom and is not afraid to share it when the time presents itself to do so.

Dedication of Purpose

The plate with the statements of purpose is held up for all to see. Each woman extends her hand toward the plate, offering a silent affirmation of what is written on the papers.

All (repeat after the leader):
We proceed into this new year with thanksgiving for what we have received. We go forward with hope. We pledge to animate the blessing that surfaced for us. We join anew with women of the world as we dedicate ourselves to personal and world transformation.

Prayer of Fastening

"Prayer fastens the soul to God."
—Julian of Norwich

Fasten my entire heart to you, Love of all Loves,
that all I am and do finds its motivation in you.

Fasten my mind to you, Inner Peace,
that whatever stirs within leads to tranquility.

Fasten my days to you, Divine Presence,
that in each happening I remain united with you.

Fasten my nights to you, Holy Darkness,
that I find restoration in your embracing silence.

Fasten my joys to you, Delight of My Soul,
that these memories comfort me in times of trouble.

Fasten my sorrows to you, Compassionate One,
that I experience solace in your kindheartedness.

Fasten my desires to you, Eternal Flame,
that my yearnings reflect the fire in your great heart.

Fasten my concerns to you, Trustworthy Confidante,
that I withdraw from my fears and place my trust in you.

Fasten my responsibilities to you, Sustainer of Strength,
that my daily efforts evolve from a non-resistant spirit.

Fasten my relationships to you, Friend of My Heart,
that your profuse love nurtures and sustains them.

Fasten my anguished world to you, Holder of Hope,
that my dreams for justice and peace become a reality.

Fasten my prayer to you, Giver of Grace,
that I might give myself ever more fully to you.

For quiet reflection

1. How sturdy is the connection that fastens me to the divine as I enter the new year?
2. How secure is the fastening to what gives my life meaning and purpose?
3. What is loose and can be sewn more tightly?
4. What needs some new thread?
5. What will I choose in this new year to keep a close bonding to that which I most value?

For sharing

Who or what in this past year has aided in fastening me to what gives my life purpose and meaning?

Who or what has helped in fastening my heart to the Holy One? (This might be a person, event or experience, a prayer, an internal nudge, a song, a work of art, nature, a ministry- or work-related situation, a family development, etc.)

Seven Gates of Transformation

This is the gate to Life;
those who know Love
shall enter through it.
— Psalm 118 (Nan C. Merrill)

Stand and face the named direction. Pause for quiet prayer after each gate is opened.

East: Let us open the gate of *Hope*,
The new beginnings, the possibilities of change and of dreams not yet lived.

South: Let us open the gate of *Compassion*,
The service we can offer, the sharing of our talents and the warmth of our hearts.

West: Let us open the gate of *Acceptance*,
The surrender asked of us, the letting go of what no longer serves our growth.

North: Let us open the gate of *Wisdom*,
The blessedness of divine guidance, readiness to use our intuition and knowledge.

Above: Let us open the gate of *Mystery*,
The vast unknown, and the secrets waiting to be revealed for our transformation.

Below: Let us open the gate of *Stability*,
That which endures and forms a firm foundation for our purpose and vision.

Within: Let us open the gate of *Divine Light*,
The radiance within each person, the light that guides, consoles, and sustains.

Prayer

Timeless One, your eternal love wraps courage around us as we enter into your invitation to further our spiritual transformation. Your ageless presence draws us to you as we step forward, ready to embrace where you lead us. Your sustaining peace rests within our every heartbeat and accompanies us into the unknown future. We bow to you with gratitude and confidence. Amen.

VESSEL OF LOVE

Introduction

On a late December day I decided to focus on being "a vessel of love" in the year ahead. To reinforce remembrance of that desire, I put a blue, glazed pottery chalice on my prayer altar. How pleased I was several weeks later when I came across a comment in Daniel Ladinsky's translation of poems by Hafiz, the Persian poet. Ladinsky describes Hafiz as being "awakened to love." Then he adds, "One cannot master love, one can only serve as a vessel of love," noting that a "glass or cup is a vessel which can often represent the human heart, or even the human being, as a vessel of love" (*A Year with Hafiz*, Daniel Ladinsky).

My desire to be this kind of vessel finds its inspiration in the two commandments that Jesus taught and lived—to love God with all our heart, mind, and soul, and to love our neighbor as our self (Mt 22:37–40). Great spiritual teachers insist that this type of love is to permeate our life at every level. It is quite easy, as Jesus noted, to love those who love us in return; but what to do with those, near or far, who determine they are our enemy?

The qualities of love found in 1 Corinthians 13:1–8 (Love is patient, kind, not jealous, pompous, or rude . . .) flow easily off the tongue of those who read them, but daily living can quickly challenge the activation of those golden words. Everyday life, however, remains the central arena in which love grows. Like the tiny droplets of wine filling a chalice, so it is with love. The little actions done with kindness, selflessness, patience, forgiveness, and respect are the droplets filling the vessel of love.

Reading: 2 Kings 4:1–7

Now the wife of a member of the company of the prophets cried to Elisha, "Your servant my husband is dead, and you know that your servant feared the Lord, but a creditor has come to take my two children as slaves." Elisha said to her, "What shall I do for you? Tell me, what do you have in the house?" She answered, "Your servant has nothing in the house, except a jar of oil." He said, "Go outside and borrow vessels from all your neighbors, empty vessels and not just a few. Then go in, and shut the door behind you and your children, and start pouring into these vessels; when each is full, set it aside." So she left him and shut the door behind her and her children; they kept bringing vessels to her, and she kept pouring. When the vessels were full, she said to her son, "Bring me another vessel." But he said to her, "There are no more." Then the oil stopped flowing. She came and told the man of God, and he said, "Go sell the oil and pay your debts, and you and your children can live on the rest."

Meditation

Hold in your hands a large, empty vessel such as a jar, a pitcher, large glass, or deep bowl.

Ponder its spaciousness, openness, and ability to be filled.

Imagine your inner self as a vessel waiting to be filled with qualities of love.

Call in virtues you most desire to fill the vessel as you embark on the new year.

Don't be afraid to call in a lot. You have plenty of room in your vessel.

(You might also want to write these virtues on small pieces of paper and place them in the vessel, drawing them out, one at a time, during January as a reminder of your desire to be a vessel of love.)

Prayer

All Encompassing Heart,
where there is impatience, let me bring kindness.
Where there is strife, let me bring harmony.
Where there is hurt, let me bring healing.
Where there is rigidity, let me bring openness.
Where there is judgment, let me bring understanding.

Wide and Spacious Love,
Turn me toward your unconditional acceptance.
I seek to be a vessel of your great love.
Let me carry your love into all parts of my life
and pour it forth willingly and generously.

Other

A Song for the Circle of Life

Sing for the spirit of women
gathered in a sacred circle;
sing for openness and dedication,
evolving purpose on a spiritual path.

Sing for the seed of self-worth
with deepening roots,
stretching upward insistently,
shedding fear, gaining strength.

Sing for the countless talents
birthing into greater wholeness,
every developed ability
a testimony to animated energy.

Sing for the struggles shared,
compassionate threads
weaving their way through wounds,
a kindness deep and wide.

Sing for the delight of pure joy,
of laughter and unmitigated fun,
dance suffused with playfulness
and passionate engagement with life.

Sing for the heart's secluded secrets
snuggled in unpretentious corners,
secrets waiting to be called forth,
aching for the confidence of voice.

Sing for the mystery held in the soul,
the melody born in every woman;
sing for this resonating beauty,
the presence of indwelling harmony.

Sing for recognition, appreciation,
honor these countless gifts.
Together evoking energizing power
emerging from kindred hearts.
Women forming a circle of life,
wisely claiming their true identity.

ENTERING A FRESH DAY OF LIFE

Imagine yourself as a diver on a cliff.
Now exhale and dive into the unscripted day.
—Mark Nepo

Unscripted. This day. My day. A fresh day. Waiting.
Ready to be opened. Holding more than what is expected.
No matter the lengthy list of have-to-do, don't-want-to-do,
Enter with a readiness to receive, to appreciate.
Prepare for a full plunge instead of a toe-in-the-water.

Release the tight grip on a measured schedule.
Stand on the threshold of dawn like a diver on a cliff
Eager to receive what awaits, ready for adventure.
Aim for the deep waters of life where the day's activity
Will surely bring an opportunity to connect with the Holy.

Even if there is a chill of morning disgruntledness
Or a hesitation about what the daunting waters hold,
Enter the approaching hours as positively as possible.
Aim toward a full-hearted dive, straight into the depths.

Draw strength while standing on the cliff of faith.
Remember the Guardian of Dawn as a steady companion.
Lean forward with courage. Let go with full confidence.
Leap with a no-holds-on. Leap without dawdling distractions.

Be willing to dive into the unwanted, as well as the welcomed.
Head into yawning humdrum, as well as the extremely exciting,
Summon awareness of being carried on Spirit's supportive wings.

Hit the water with gusto, no matter how dreaded the entrance.
Upon arrival, swim with total confidence and eagerness,
Liberated for a while from self-imposed drudgery of past days.
Float along now, buoyed by renewed trust and gratefulness.

And when the next day dawns, stand on the cliff of faith again,
With even more assurance, with even more trusted anticipation
Than the day before. Stand on the cliff's solid stone of prayer.
Get ready for the dive.

EUCHARIST

Eucharist comes in many forms.
Yesterday at dawn I stepped
onto the round, white stones
of Lake Michigan's vast shore;
I felt the deepest communion
with all that exists, especially
with the One who woos my heart.
I thought of my friend, Janet,
holding out her open hands at Mass
to receive the Gift she holds dear.
Today, as the retreat house bell
calls the women to come receive,
I stand before the full-bodied,
incandescent maple tree, sunshine
illuminating its golden leaves
like a host held high in the blue sky.
I stand in creation's communion line,
bow my head, open my heart,
and receive Eucharist once again.

LABYRINTH PRAYER

You are with me, Ever-Present Journeyer, as I stand at the opening to the labyrinth. Many times I have stood unsure at the entrance of an unknown journey in my life. Remind me that I do not make the passage to the center alone. You accompany my every footstep.

Encourage me to bring my entire life with me—whatever encumbers and inhibits, whatever enthuses and inspires. No part of my life can be left behind. Each particle is woven into my relationship with you. I bring all of it onto the path that draws me inward and forward.

Instill trust in me as I begin to walk the back and forth movements of the path taking me further and deeper into the mystery of you and into the unknown recesses of my soul. Assure me that I can walk without fear, knowing you are my Guide. Whatever truth awaits, it will be given when I am available and ready to receive it.

Slow me with your stillness so I do not hurry the steps I take. Enable my patience and mindfulness to assist my focus on each step, as I join my breath to you, the One Breath.

When I reach the center of the labyrinth open the portals of my mind and heart to remove anything that prevents me from seeing clearly. Grant wisdom to know what to leave behind in the center. Whatever keeps me bound, unbind. Whatever holds me back, release. Whatever yearns to be set free, liberate.

Before I begin the journey leading out of the labyrinth, place in my heart the gift that will support my being more truly yours. Restore what has been neglected. Refresh what has grown stale. Rejoice what has saddened. Reenergize what has drooped with weariness.

As I make my way from the center strengthen and deepen my commitment to personal and world transformation. May each step be a step of kindness, a step of compassion, a step of justice, a step of hope, until I reach the last step that moves me out beyond the labyrinth.

Wrap your peace around me as I go forth. May I move into what lies ahead with restored confidence, reassured of my desire and ability to be a person of great love.

Reading Paul Zimmer's Poetry

The summer I came across
Zimmer's poetry
I needed his humor,
and his easy way of saying
what is deep
in every human heart.
I needed his words
to remind me
that life yearns to be caressed,
not managed
like some wayward cow
in a milking stall.
Zimmer's poetry led me
back to my own heart
where all along she waited
to tell me how precious
is the unfolding
of life's meandering.

SUMMER PRAYER OF INNER PEACE

Our inner sanctuary of peacefulness often diminishes in the flurry of summer's social activities, with endless tasks remaining unfinished at home, the return from vacation to numerous deadlines and pressures of work. When this happens, our internal direction and sense of purpose easily upends itself. If we lack attentiveness, our ability to live out of our best self tends to lessen. Now is the time to restore an awareness of the magnificent temple within us where the Spirit of Peace abides. We can return to this calm, abiding presence whenever we deliberately choose to do so. May the following prayer be a source of remembering and tending to this indwelling gift.

Peaceful Presence,
Grant me the courage to slow down the hurried pace of life in order to be mindful of your ever-present guidance and assistance, especially when I try to go it alone.

Restore my perception of the inherent joy that awaits me in each day if only I turn toward you with a recognition of your vibrant energy moving through me.

Awaken me to a keener awareness of your light-filled presence within my being, especially when life fills with shadows of sadness and the cloudiness of concerns.

Show me how you are dwelling in those places of my life where I've forgotten to welcome you with an open heart of acceptance and hospitality.

Interrupt my self-defeating schemes and desires so I have a keener sense of how they lead me further from you and obliterate inner peace.

When you move me toward change and deeper relationship with you, show me where my resistance to that growth-filled invitation resides.

Enliven my physical senses to the beauty and wonder of ordinary moments and a resounding gratitude for your presence within those moments.

Shake free what keeps my thoughts and feelings imprisoned in anxiety and useless fretting.

Draw me into the stillness essential for your serenity to dwell in my being, and lead me into times of solitude, even if you have to drag me there.

Come, tickle my mind and heart into restored peacefulness so I more readily and wisely welcome you to the home of my heart.

Tapping of the Heart

Introduction: from *Abide*, Macrina Wiederkehr

In his book *The Heart of the Hunter*, Laurens van der Post tells his story of living in the Kalahari Desert with the bushmen of South Africa. It became obvious to van der Post that these primitive peoples knew intimately the presence of wisdom in every blade of grass and in every heartbeat. The bushmen had a mysterious kind of inner knowing. They knew when the enemy was approaching and danger was near. They knew when to move their camps, and when and where the rains would come. They knew where to go for hunting that would sustain their lives. When questioned about this mysterious inner knowledge, they spoke of what they called "the tapping of the heart."

From an early age, they had been commanded to heed this tapping. When they felt it coming, they were to become very quiet inside and to listen vigilantly to the tapping. It was like a sixth sense, an unexplainable knowing. Reflecting on the uncomplicated lives of these ancient peoples, I have come to believe that this mysterious knowing in them was nothing less than the wisdom of God. . . .

We have a mystical, compelling presence within—the Spirit of Jesus dwelling in the depths of our beings. Surely, we too can learn to attend the tapping of the heart, which is the wisdom of God revealing itself to us in the deepening places of our lives.

Namasté. I greet the depths of Divine Wisdom in you.

Reading: 1 Corinthians 2:9–12

As it is written, "What no eye has seen, nor ear heard, nor the human heart conceived, what God has prepared for those who love him" —these things God has revealed to us through the Spirit; for the Spirit searches everything, even the depths of God. For what human being knows what is truly human except the human spirit that is within . . . Now we have received not the spirit of the world but the Spirit that is from God so that we may understand the gifts bestowed on us by God.

Pause for a mindful resting in the Spirit's presence. Listen for what may be tapping on your heart.

Integrative Prayer: "Tapping Ourselves Awake"

We tap various parts of our body to remind us that our entire being is open to the Spirit of Wisdom. Tap three times on the particular part of the body after it is mentioned. On the third tap, allow at least a fifteen second pause to be present to that part of the body.

Forehead: We seek knowledge of Divine Wisdom through our mind and its revelations.

Ears: We discover Divine Wisdom through the internal sounds and silences of our being.

Eyes: We look closely to recognize how Divine Wisdom reveals through others.

Nose: We attend to the rhythm of our breath knowing Divine Wisdom breathes in us.

Mouth: We speak with courage and kindness and find Divine Wisdom in our words.

Skin: We become aware of Divine Wisdom's love through touching and being touched.

Shoulders: We experience Divine Wisdom's strength when we carry heavy concerns.

Belly: We acknowledge the stirring of Divine Wisdom as we attend to our emotions.

Feet: We walk along in daily life and heed Divine Wisdom's guidance in each place.

Hands: We open our hands as a sign of our desire to share Divine Wisdom's benefits.

Heart: We welcome the unbounded love of Divine Wisdom in the depths of our being.

Closing

Those gathered speak the following words about Divine Wisdom from the Wisdom of Solomon (Wisdom 7:24–28):

> She is a breath of the power of God,
> and a pure emanation of the glory of the Almighty;
> therefore nothing defiled gains entrance into her.
> For she is a reflection of eternal light,
> a spotless mirror of the working of God,
> and an image of (God's) goodness.
> In every generation she passes into holy souls
> and makes them friends of God and prophets;
> for God loves nothing so much
> as the person who lives with wisdom.

Tapping the Heart

*Each one present is now invited once more to tap three times on his/her heart. These words are spoken aloud after each tap: **Divine Wisdom, I am listening to you**.*

THE GLIMPSE

Walking the autumn corridors
of Raccoon River Park,
wet leaves sticking to my shoes,
cool wind dancing on my face.
my mind lost in work left behind
heaped on the office desk.

Walking on the wooded path
eyes glazed and un-seeing,
abruptly alerted to swift movement,
the flash of wide, gray-blue wings
sweeping upward and away
leaving only a faint trace
of presence in my mind's eye,

I sought, looked then, intently,
but the precious moment escaped,
the bird, possibly a large, blue heron,
moving on, far beyond my sight.

"If only" I had been mindful,
lived fully in the present moment,
allowed the beauty of the bird
to envelop and carry me along
through the unattended work.

"If only" —

Instead, I returned with a heavy regret,
but also with keen resolution,
to be with what is, when it is,
awake and open to the unexpected,
allowing life to charm me with sudden delight.

THE QUESTION

Endlessly, from dawn until long after day has closed
its sleepy eyes, the tiny house wren voices
his aching song, an energetic warble filled with passion,
calling, calling, calling, stopping the persistent message
only briefly, hurrying to carry thin twigs
with unmitigated resolve, creating the nesting place
for his anticipated love.

What or who, I ask myself every day, stirs so endlessly
within me that I am equally passionate and devoted?
Have I ever been that zealous, that focused, that intent
on the Eternal Love of my deepest being, so much so
that each syllable birthed from my soul goes forward
as a fervent cry of endless affection to the One I desire?

On and on the wren's unceasing supplication enters
each opened window of my home and heart.
On and on the question of "who or what" lingers
with each heartbeat of the day, like the dedicated
song of this plain brown bird, waiting faithfully
to be acknowledged.

UNNAMABLE GOD

Unnamable God, I feel you
with me at every moment.
You are my food, my drink,
my sunlight, and the air I breathe.
—Psalm 16 (Stephen Mitchell)

with each refreshing rain
each slant of sunshine
each beam of moonlight
each whisper of wind

in every spiraling thought
every turning of the heart
every spoken and written word
every action large and small

you steady, you lead
you encourage, you guide
you embrace, you never let go

one with my soul, one with my life
one with me in the first breath
one with me in the last

you know me now
you will know me
always and forever

I remember
I rejoice

Untangle the Nets

The aim of spiritual practice,
no matter its form,
is to untangle the nets that living snares us in.
—Mark Nepo

When we are caught in the web of disagreements and the snares of hostilities that are difficult to mend, may we give ourselves to the effort of untangling the nets of conflict.

When we find ourselves caught up in an overly full schedule and way too much to do, may we find wisdom and courage to pause and loosen the knots of our hurried life.

When we ignore or neglect our fatigue, illness, or pain, may we untangle the net of ignoring our physical self and respond with care.

When we find our faith or spiritual life entwined with indifference or disregard, may we disentangle the knots and repair what needs mending.

When we lose our hope for peace because of the world's endless pain and suffering, may we lean on divine compassion and continue to loosen the knots of hopelessness that seep into our hearts.

Divine Untangler, you know the journey each of us is on. Remind us often that the slower we are to untangle the net, the harder it is to unravel. Help us to accept and grow beyond any part of our life where the net is too twisted to be undone. Grant us the courage to untie what is possible. In all areas of our lives, may we "learn the patience of the fisherman, trying to see what is tangled" and then, to "slowly and gently undo the knots, one by one. All to make the web whole again." Amen.

Quotes attributed to Mark Nepo.

Pentecost

Breath of Life

~

Introduction: from *Breath of Life*, Denis Edwards

Read by the leader or another member of the group.

The immanent breath of God is always in communion with the Word and the Source of All. . . . [I]t is the Spirit's role to dwell in creatures, creating the bond of communion between the creature and the life of God . . . The Breath of God escapes the limits of the human and embraces the universe and infinitely more. The Spirit is the presence of God at the heart of the universe, a mysterious presence that fills the whole universe yet is intimately interior to each creature.

Leader: Let us stand and greet one another in silence.

Take a deep breath. Let it out slowly. Look at each one with reverence and awe, noting the communion shared through breathing together. Pause to be with the reality of both bodily breath and the divine breath drawing one another into an invisible, strengthening union.

Song

"O Living Breath of God," *Seven Sacred Pauses*, Velma Frye.

Prayers

Jesus said, "The wind blows where it chooses and you hear the sound of it, but you do not know where it comes from or where it goes. So it is with everyone who is born of the Spirit." (Jn 3:8)

Mysterious One, you move me on the winds of your love. You sail with me on the clouds of my uncertainty. You stay with me in the toughest of threatening storms. You whisper in the winds of my searching, so silent at times I wonder if and where you might abide. Ever present, ever elusive, I cannot control or define your interacting essence. Yet you continually draw me to your heart with each breath I take. You ask only that I surrender my desire to regulate and manage how you move and reveal yourself to me.

The Spirit of God has made me, and the breath of the Almighty gives me life. (Jb 33:4)

Creator, your breath slipped graciously into my birthing body and brought me forth into life on this planet. With each breath I have taken since coming forth from my mother's womb your Spirit has breathed within me. With every inhalation and exhalation of my physical form your Spirit urges a strengthened union with you. May I continue to respond to your grace-filled presence until the day I take my last physical breath and unite fully with you, the One Breath.

When the day of Pentecost had come, they were all together in one place. And suddenly from heaven there came a sound like the rush of a violent wind, and it filled the entire house where they were sitting. . . . All of them were filled with the Holy Spirit. (Acts 2:1–2, 4a)

Spirit of Community, remind me that my life with you is most often found in the midst of others in whom you live and move and have your being. Your intermingling presence unites me with all living beings. You permeate the space within and between those with whom I engage. You rush in where I least expect. You surprise me with the beauty of your love and your eager passion to change systems and sources that oppress. Ignite my love. Hasten my actions for social justice. Open the doors of my mind and heart so you can fill the entire house of my being with your all-embracing love.

Thus says the Lord God to these bones: I will cause breath to enter you and you shall live. (Ez 37:5)

Giver of Life, your Spirit reaches into the brittle bones of my relationships, enters the dried substance of my prayer, and filters through the withered membranes of my forsaken hope. I wait with patience when I sink into these dehydrated places. I trust that your loving Breath spreads through whatever becomes parched with distractions and unwanted occurrences. I believe you will restore these dried aspects of my inner life with renewed vitality.

Song

Sing the chant "Spirit Come," *Out of the Ordinary*, Joyce Rupp.

Spirit, Spirit, come into my life.
Spirit, Spirit, come into my life.
Fill me, change me, let me hear your voice.
Spirit, Spirit, come into my life.

Meditation

Sit and be attentive to the pattern of breathing, the natural movement of inhalation and exhalation, the in and out rhythm of this physical gift of life. Enter into quiet meditation using the following breath prayer:

Breathe in . . . the grace-filled, life-giving Spirit of the Creator.
Breathe out . . . this Love to individuals, groups of people, creatures, to all on our planet who are in need of the Holy Spirit's vibrant, transforming presence.

Prayer

Together:

Spirit of the Universe, Spirit of my heart, I welcome you into my life.
Come visit the places within me where Love has yet to find a dwelling place.
Breathe within all of my existence with the power of your transforming grace.
I open my entire being to you and thank you for the gift of your presence.
Amen.

ESSENCE OF LOVE

Evidence everywhere in my history,
I have been inspired, drawn, carried,
assured, enticed, comforted, nudged.
Now in this stage of our relationship
you move in the depths of my being,
blend in with the thoughts of my mind,
intermingle in my heart's every beat.
Always you invite me to be true,
to approach life with quiet integrity.

Essence of Love, Spirit, Encourager,
I can name you in limitless ways;
it makes no difference the title.
What counts is my trust in your closeness,
my response to your intrinsic request
to be peace-bringer and holder-of-dreams.

Holy Wisdom, Breath of the Soul,
you are my Pentecost, the winged one
who rests in the hollow of my being,
moving gracefully, faithfully, in the depths.

My Beloved Companion, Steadfast Guide,
Eternal Beckoner, Restorer of Life,
I am indebted forever to your presence.
I place my trust in you once again
as the breath of your love goes forth.

FILLED WITH THE FIRE OF LOVE

Kindle the lamp of love
with your life.
—Rabindranth Tagore

Namasté. I greet the Fire of Love within you.

Reading: Galatians 5:22–26

After each of the following fruits of the Spirit are named, a candle is lit. All those gathered respond after each candle is lit:

"If we live by the Spirit, let us also be guided by the Spirit" (Gal 5:25).
Leader:
Let the fire of *love* be aflame in our hearts and in our lives.
Let the fire of *joy* be aflame in our hearts and in our lives.
Let the fire of *peace* be aflame in our hearts and in our lives.
Let the fire of *patience* be aflame in our hearts and in our lives.
Let the fire of *kindness* be aflame in our hearts and in our lives.
Let the fire of *generosity* be aflame in our hearts and in our lives.
Let the fire of *faithfulness* be aflame in our hearts and in our lives.
Let the fire of *gentleness* be aflame in our hearts and in our lives.
Let the fire of *self-control* be aflame in our hearts and in our lives.

Song

"Sacred Fire," *Melodies of the Universe*, Jan Novotka.
Leader: Let us reflect quietly on how the Fire of Love is aflame in our lives.

Prayer

Flame of Love, Enkindler of Hearts, enlighten my mind to recognize where my love has grown dim. Spark renewed desire in my heart to give myself ever more completely to your service. Beam your grace through my being so I respond freely. May the fruits of your love be harvested through me. I will share them generously. Amen.

PENTECOST PRAYER

And suddenly from heaven there came a sound
like the rush of a violent wind,
and it filled the entire house where they were sitting.
All of them were filled with the Holy Spirit.
—Acts 2:2, 4

Spirit, Wild One
sweeping in, unseen, unannounced,
unexpected, uncompromising,
pressing through the door
startling those hovering in fear
shaking them out of the corners,
awakening concealed gifts.

Spirit, Wild One,
relentless loving presence,
bringing strength to the weak,
courage to the fearful,
determination to the doubtful,
joy to the disheartened,
faith to the disbelieving.

Spirit, Wild One,
come whirling into my soul space,
gather what remains in disarray,
lift up what is neglected,
send forth what wants to hold back,
impassion what hesitates,
heal what remains wounded.

Spirit, Wild One,
breathe large gusts in me,
sweep through my being,
drench me with hope,
soften my resistance,

wrap your love around me
until I welcome you fully.

Thanksgiving

ABUNDANCE

~

May God give you of the dew of heaven,
And of the fatness of the earth,
and plenty of grain and wine.
—Genesis 27:28

A variety of seeds are in a basket and also scattered upon a cloth on the prayer table.

Introduction

Now is the time of harvest when Earth's generosity is evident everywhere. Plants often produce some sort of seed when they reach maturation. The production of these seeds manifests as a metaphor for both the abundance of the current season and a positive anticipation of the future. The dictionary describes "abundance" as an extremely plentiful or overly sufficient quantity or supply; an overflowing fullness; or affluence, wealth.

We are reminded of the spiritual and physical abundance given to us by the Holy One in the following scripture verses:

"I came that they may have life, and have it abundantly." (Jn 10:10)

The meek shall inherit the land,
And delight themselves in abundant prosperity. (Ps 37:11)

Mortals ate the bread of angels,
(The Holy One) sent them food in abundance. (Ps 78:25)

Namasté. I greet the Bountiful Harvest in you.

Reading 1: from *The Heart of the New Thought*, Ella Wheeler Wilcox

Not until you obtain the faculty of being happy through your spiritual and mental faculties, independent of material conditions, not until you learn to value wealth only as a means of helpfulness, can you safely turn your powers of concentration upon the idea of opulence. . . . Make . . . your assertion of opulence the last in your list, as you make Love first. Call unto yourself spiritual insight, absolute unselfishness, desire for universal good, wisdom, justice, and usefulness, and last of all opulence. Think of yourself as possessed of all these qualities before you picture financial independence. For without love for your kind, without the desire for usefulness and the spiritual insight and the wisdom to be just before being generous, your money would bring you only temporary pleasure, and would do the world no good.

Reading 2: from *The Tao of Abundance*, Laurence Boldt

No individual operates in a vacuum. It would be absurd to deny the impact that the values and organization of the broader society have on us as individuals. In an effort to secure the ever-expanding productivity and consumption upon which its "health" depends, modern commercial culture vigorously promotes a "lack consciousness." We buy things we don't need (or even want), because we have become convinced that we will be somehow lacking or inferior without them. We do work we don't want to do, because we have become convinced that there is a scarcity of good jobs and that we can't create our own work. Thus, even while we amass more and more stuff, the feeling of abundance keeps eluding us. In addition to the role that the values of the broader society have in promoting a psychology of lack within the individual, the current organization of society poses institutional barriers to his or her creative development and financial independence.

Reading 3: from *Let Your Life Speak*, Parker Palmer

Daily I am astonished at how readily I believe that something I need is in short supply. If I hoard possessions, it is because I believe that there are not enough to go around. . . . The irony, often tragic, is that by embracing the scarcity assumption, we create the very scarcities we fear. If I hoard material goods, others will have too little and I will never have enough. If I fight my way up the ladder of power, others will be defeated and I will never be secure. If I get jealous of someone I love, I am likely to drive that person away. If I cling to the words I have written as if they were the last of their kind, the pool of new possibilities will surely go dry. We create scarcity by fearfully accepting it as law, and by competing with others for resources as if we were stranded on the Sahara at the last oasis.

Quiet Reflection

If I could describe my experience of abundance what would I include?

Time to Share

The Basket of Abundance

> *Each person is given a small piece of paper on which to write five central words that name their abundance.*
>
> *The basket of seeds is passed around. As each one places his or her paper in the basket, the group responds with this blessing:* **Thank you for the spiritual harvest of your life.**

Closing

"The Second Giving"

The second giving of God is the great giving
out of the portions of the seraphim,
abundances with which the soul is laden
once it has given up all things for Him.

The second growth of God is the rich growing,
with fruits no constant gathering can remove,
the flourishing of those who by God's mercy
have cut themselves down to the roots for love.

God seeks a heart with bold and boundless hungers
that sees itself and earth as paltry stuff;
God loves a soul that casts down all He gave it
and stands and cries that it was not enough.
                                        —Jessica Powers

Together: The might of your awesome deeds shall be proclaimed,
and I will declare your greatness.
They shall celebrate the fame of your abundant goodness (Ps 145:6–7).

Bringing in the Harvest

~

"I appointed you to go and bear fruit,
fruit that will last."

—John 15:16

An empty cornucopia, basket, or other container associated with harvest time is placed in the center of the group. Various fruits, grains, and vegetables harvested from the local area are either brought to the ritual by those present or placed around the empty object by the prayer leader.

Introduction

This is the time of harvesting fruits, vegetables, and grains of the land. We come together in gratitude for the diversity and richness of what our good earth allows us to grow and produce for creaturely consumption. We also gather in gratitude for what our Creator grows and produces within our interior land, those virtues and positive qualities we have nurtured in our spirits. An abundance of fruitfulness resides among us. Let us draw encouragement from one another's harvest and rejoice in the maturation of the Holy One's love.

Prayer

Sower of Seeds, you have planted in our hearts the potential for many gifts of your love to grow and ripen. Charity, authenticity, mercy, honesty, humility, forgiveness, loyalty, patience, understanding, courage, kindness, faith, respect, and other qualities reflective of your goodness dwell in our interior fields and garden. We gather here to recall what has grown and matured. We exult in the diversity and richness of our inner harvest and offer you our gratitude.

Quiet Meditation

Each one present reflects on a specific quality or virtue that has increased since last harvest time, including a specific situation that led to this further maturation.

Sharing

The group is invited to name the virtue or quality and tell the story of how this feature continues to mature in his or her life. After the sharing each chooses a fruit, grain, or vegetable and places it in the container as a confirmation of what he or she has described.

Closing Prayer

Each person calls out the virtue or quality he or she shared. After each is named the group responds: **We rejoice in your harvest. Continue to be bountiful.**

GENEROUS LOVE

We assemble here in this circle of prayer and celebration, joined as one through the bountiful love of an Unseen Presence. We acknowledge the generosity of this amazing divinity who continually relates to us with a kindness that knows no bounds.

Chant between each segment:

Holy One, O Holy One dwelling within me (from *Out of the Ordinary*, Joyce Rupp).

See what love the Father has given us (1 Jn 3:1).

> Bestower of our spiritual wealth,
> how awesome is the immensity of your love.
> Praise to you for the endless outpouring of your grace.
> Blessed are you, Extravagant Source of Life,
> your boundless beauty and unlimited benevolence
> anoints us at every moment of our existence.

All: **Holy One, O Holy One dwelling within me**

Let them return . . . to our God [who] will abundantly pardon (Is 55:7b).

> We are seekers of you, the Mystery we name as God.
> We are disciples of Jesus, our beloved friend and teacher
> whom you sent to us from the fullness of your love.
> When we look at how he lived and what he taught,
> we see the depth and breadth of divine generosity.
> We come to know this bounteous love in our own lives
> each time we turn to seek your mercy and forgiveness.

All: **Holy One, O Holy One dwelling within me**

God is able to provide you with every blessing in abundance (2 Cor 9:8).

> Generous Benefactor, you give us sufficient for our journey
> even if it does not include everything we want or expect.

Help us to recognize our plenitude and be satisfied.
Turn us away from obstacles of comparison, competition, and envy.
Strengthen our spontaneous gratitude for what we have received.

All: **Holy One, O Holy One dwelling within me**

But take care . . . so as neither to forget the things that your eyes have seen nor to let them slip from your mind all the days of your life; make them known to your children and to your children's children (Dt 4:9).

> The spiritual richness coming to us from our ancestors
> is a source of both inspiration and encouragement.
> With thankfulness, we remember those who have gone before us,
> all those who lived a life of generous love and kindness.
> We unite with both the canonized and un-canonized saints
> who gifted us personally and communally with their goodness.

All: **Holy One, O Holy One dwelling within me**

What shall I return to the Lord for all [God's] bounty to me? (Ps 116:12).

> Each of us has come forth from you, our Source of Generosity.
> Although distinct in our differences, we share oneness through you.
> In spite of this unity, a vast inequity exists among the human community.
> Aware of injustice and continued indifference to human need,
> we pray to be generous with others in our acceptance of them
> and in the sharing of both our spiritual and material resources.

All: **Holy One, O Holy One dwelling within me**

God's love has been poured into our hearts through the Holy Spirit that has been given to us (Rom 5:5).

> We remember the profuse love pouring forth from the heart of Jesus
> the night before his death when he sat at table with his friends,
> as he held the blessed bread and wine and shared it with them.
> Those he held dear were nourished with this generous gift of love.
> We trust that this profusion of love is pouring forth into our hearts now.

We re-align our intentions to share this Love with similar generosity. We pause to give thanks . . .

All: **Holy One, O Holy One dwelling within me**

To conclude, let us offer one another peace, a sign of our generous love.

O Taste and See

Introduction: from *Seven Thousand Ways to Listen*,
Mark Nepo

Leader: Grandfather Mantis eats honeycombs. Now, honey itself is that sweet thickness produced by bees from the nectar of flowers. Thousands of bees belonging to a hive gather the nectar from thousands of flowers blooming in the spring. They then bring that nectar back to the hive where, in the center, they create honey. In the center of the hive, they store the honey in an amazingly thin-walled honeycomb that they construct of beeswax.

So when Grandfather Mantis eats honeycombs to strengthen his body and think clearly, he is eating this entire process. He is eating the flowers breaking ground on the other side of winter and the nectar forming in the heart of every flower. He is eating the search of a thousand bees scenting after the nectar and their bringing it back to the center of the hive. He is eating the mysterious way they turn that nectar into honey and the hive's industry at turning their wax into a honeycomb. He is surrendering to the fact that, in order to be strong and clear, we need to internalize the unending way that the variety of life is tripped upon and gathered and worked into one thick sweetness.

Remembering

Response after each: **O taste and see the goodness of our Creator**.

We remember the beauty of our world, how all is interdependent,
like bees in a hive, each part reliant on another part in order to exist.

We remember how the Holy One resides within and among us,
energizing our love and encouraging our actions for good.

We remember the many times we have been weary and lacked enthusiasm,
how our vitality of body and spirit received needed restoration.

We remember people who are like nurturing honeycombs to us,
offering the sweetness of their enduring affection and acceptance.

We remember faith that nourishes us in times of uncertainty and difficulty, filling us with the courage to go on, much like bees sipping honey from flowers and bringing it home to the hive.

We remember the sustaining energy of nature, its ability to urge us to change, the sweet taste of the seasons as they beckon us with their transitional beauty.

We remember times when the pain of our life was gradually transformed into the sweet nectar of compassion.

We remember the wonder of our minds, all we are given in thought, insight, and decision-making, our mental faculties that lead to greater well-being.

We remember our gatherings in prayer, the strength these moments give us for our spiritual paths, the energizing inspiration we gain to be our best selves.

Prayer

Together: O Sweet Taste of Goodness, how numerous are the ways you enrich and invigorate our lives. Thank you, especially, for those who provide opportunities and encouragement. For it is most often through our relationship with others that we gather the necessary nectar for our growth. Remind us often of the process of honey-making as a metaphor for the spiritual transformation that can be ours. Come, visit the honeycomb of our spirits and teach us anew how to grow. We turn to you with gratitude for your guidance. Amen.

Transitions

Leave-Taking Blessing

Leader: Let us turn our hearts to the presence of the Divine Journeyer who accompanied Abraham and Sarah, Mary and Joseph, and many other biblical ancestors. They held in their hearts a deep faith that this Companion would not abandon them, that they would be sheltered in the peace of divine guidance. We join our hearts with _____ in blessing him (her) as he (she) prepares to journey forth from here.

Steady and Trustworthy Guide of our journeys, we celebrate the goodness of _____ and ask your blessing as he (she) continues on the road of life. May the love and gratitude in our hearts be a bond that unites us forever, wherever we may be. We thank you for the gifts we have received from _____'s presence during our time together.

Let us now mention qualities of _____ and experiences for which for which we are grateful.

Those gathered now name qualities of the person who is leaving.

Blessing

Response after each: **Go with courage. Go with trust. Go with our love to support you.**

Forehead
May you be blessed with constant hope,
with confidence in what awaits you,
and a strong trust that all shall be well.

Heart
May you be blessed with bounteous love,
with many surprises of renewed friendship,
and with an ever deepening love of the Holy One.

Hands
May you be blessed with graced surrender
to let go of what keeps you from growing,
to learn from the obstacles that arise,
and to live each day with a spirit of openness.

Feet
May you be blessed with courage
to stand strong in adversity,
to wait with patience for what you need,
and to look forward to the new growth awaiting you.

All: **Go in peace with our love and gratitude alive in you as you depart.**

Moving to a Nursing Home

[God] will keep your going out and your coming in
from this time on and forevermore.
—Psalm 121:8

Blessing of the Shawl

May this shawl be a source of comfort and warmth, an assurance of God's shelter. May this shawl be a mantle of protection from discouragement and a reminder of all those who embraced you with friendship and love in the past. May this shawl be a provider of contentment, a haven of rest and relaxation.

Remembering the Refuge and Shelter of God

The Lord is my light and my salvation: whom shall I fear?
The Lord is the stronghold of my life; of whom shall I be afraid?

For he will hide me in his shelter
in the day of trouble;
he will conceal me under the cover of his tent;
he will set me high on a rock.
—Psalm 27:1, 5

The shawl is placed around the future nursing home resident.

We place this prayer shawl around you. We bless you with our prayers and love.

Response between each of the following blessings:
Shelter her (him) under your wings.

May you be wrapped in the tender presence of God, who holds you close as you enter this passage of your life.

May you be wrapped in the quiet serenity of God when you are weary and sleepiness overtakes your desire to be more active.

May you be wrapped in the assuring guidance of God's care when you feel like you have lost your way.

May you be wrapped in the welcoming joy of God when you long for companionship and enjoyment in your new residence.

May you be wrapped in the providence of God when you find yourself longing for things you left behind and no longer have with you.

May you be wrapped in the spirit of God's empowerment when you need courage and strength to adapt to your changed environment.

May you be wrapped in the compassion of God when you experience thoughts and feelings that bring a sense of loss and sadness.

May you be wrapped in the strength of God, who will uphold you when you experience your physical limitations.

May you be wrapped in the love of God, who knows the difficulties and challenges of this important transition.

All: When you wrap this prayer shawl around you, remember that our prayers encircle you with care. Your presence will be a blessing to those whom your life touches in your new residence. God will watch over you and keep you safe. Amen.

THE GATE OF TRANSITION

Happy is the one who listens to me,
watching daily at my gates,
waiting beside my doors.
—Proverbs 8:34

Choose a comfortable posture.
Breathe calmly until you sense a stillness within you.
Encourage peace to flow through your being.
Set aside apprehensions, uncertainties, and questions about the future.
Let go of anything that keeps you from focusing on the present moment.
Remember the abiding presence of Holy Wisdom.
Pray for openness to welcome this assuring assistance.

In this attentive, relaxed state, the image of a gate comes to your mind.
It can be any kind of gate. Let it appear in your imagination.
Where is the gate?
What shape is it?
What is the material? (Wood? Metal? Stone? Glass? Something else?)
What color is the gate?
Are there any designs on it? Any words or a message?
How does it open and close? Does it have a latch or a lock?

This is the gate of your current transition.
It leads to what evolves for you in the future.
Walk quietly, slowly, up to the gate.
Someone waits there for you: Holy Wisdom in disguise.
You move closer and sit down to join this guiding presence.

Sense the confidence that Holy Wisdom instills in you.
Notice the gaze of assuring love moving toward you.
Speak about your thoughts and feelings regarding your transition.
Ask for direction in knowing how best to proceed.
What will most assist you as you move onward?
Is there a message that you receive from Holy Wisdom?

Remain by this gate for however long you wish.
See yourself standing up when your time seems complete.
Tuck the guidance you've received into your heart.
Go forth from the gate with your hand in Holy Wisdom's hand.
See the two of you moving forward to a place of serenity.

Let your mind focus on this scene until the two of you are in the far distance.
Go forth from your meditation with peace and trust resting within you.

In Times of Uncertainty

Holy Maker of Moonlight
Singing through starlight
Keeper of all life
Hidden Seed
deep in the soil of the earth
Fertile Ground, Womb of the Night
bring us new birth
—Sara Thomsen

Namasté. I greet the Creator of Transformation in you.

Song

"Darkness Cover Me," *Fertile Ground*, Sara Thomsen.

Reading 1: from *Comfortable with Uncertainty*, Pema Chodron

The first noble truth says that it's part of being human to feel discomfort. All around us the wind, the fire, the earth, the water, are always taking on different qualities: they're like magicians. We also change like the weather. We ebb and flow like the tides. We wax and wane like the moon. We fail to see that like the weather, we are fluid, not solid. And so we suffer.

Reading 2: Matthew 6:25–27

"Therefore I tell you, do not worry about your life, what you will eat or what you will drink, or about your body, what you will wear. Is not life more than food, and the body more than clothing? Look at the birds of the air. They neither sow nor reap nor gather into barns, and yet your heavenly Father feeds them. Are you not of more value than they? And can any of you by worrying add a single hour to your span of life?"

Meditation

What in my life feels uncomfortable, uncertain, unpredictable?
Is there anything I am resisting or insisting be changed?
How am I responding to this?
How might I approach the unwanted aspects of my life so I turn *with* them, rather than push *against* them?
How might I worry less and trust more?

Stepping into the Darkness

Stand in a circle. The leader reads the following intentions. The group repeats them as they take one step forward with each of the intentions.

I intend to walk confidently through darkness / with belief in my ability to thrive amid uncertainty.

I intend to walk confidently through darkness / no matter how fluid and foggy my life feels.

I intend to walk confidently through darkness / and set aside what keeps me from loving self and others.

I intend to walk confidently through darkness / trusting I have guides aplenty to help me find my way.

I intend to walk confidently though darkness / with freedom to ebb and flow like the tides.

I intend to walk confidently through darkness / and not give in to fear or worry.

I intend to walk confidently through darkness / believing I have strength enough to face any resistance.

I intend to walk confidently through darkness / being still as a mountain, / resting in the trust that all shall be well.

Song

"Turning Toward the Morning," *Turning Toward the Morning*, Gordon Bok.

References

Barbour, Julian. *The End of Time*. New York: Oxford University Press, 2001.

Boldt, Laurence. *The Tao of Abundance*. New York: Penguin Books, 1999.

Chodron, Pema. *Comfortable with Uncertainty*. Boulder, CO: Shambhala Publications, 2003.

Chopra, Deepak. "The Law of Giving." Chapter 2 in *Seven Spiritual Laws of Success*. Novato, CA: New World Library, 1994.

Delio, Ilia. *The Unbearable Wholeness of Being*. Maryknoll, NY: Orbis Books, 2013.

Edwards, Denis. *Breath of Life*. Maryknoll, NY: Orbis Books, 2004.

Ferder, Fran. *Enter the Story*. Maryknoll, NY: Orbis Books, 2010.

Fox, John. *Finding What You Didn't Lose*. New York: TarcherPerigee, 1995.

Guenther, Margaret. *Holy Listening*. Cambridge, MA: Cowley Publications, 1992.

Harvey, Andrew. *The Way of Passion*. New York: TarcherPerigee, 2000.

Hillisum, Etty. *An Interrupted Life*. Translated by Arnold J. Pomerans. New York: Henry Holt and Co., 1996.

Julian of Norwich. *Enfolded in Love: Daily Readings with Julian of Norwich*. New York: Seabury Press, 1980.

Kornfield, Jack. *A Path with Heart*. New York: Bantam, 1993.

Ladinsky, Daniel. *A Year with Hafiz*. New York: Penguin Books, 2011.

Livingston, Patricia. "Meditation" (January 6, 2015). *Living with Christ* 16, no. 1.

Main, John. *Word into Silence*. London: Canterbury Press, 2006, quoted in *The Way of Silence*, by David Steindl-Rast. Cincinnati, OH: Franciscan Media, 2016.

McCormick, Patrick. "Just the Right Touch," *U.S. Catholic*, June 1999, 46–48.

Merrill, Nan C. *Psalms for Praying*. New York: Continuum, 2001.

Mitchell, Stephen. *A Book of Psalms*, New York: HarperPerennial, 1894.

Nepo, Mark. *Seven Thousand Ways to Listen*. New York: Altria Books, 2013.

O'Donohue, John. *To Bless the Space Between Us*. New York: Doubleday, 2008.

Orsborn, Carol. *The Art of Resilience*. New York: Three Rivers Press, 1997.

Palmer, Parker. *A Hidden Wholeness*. San Francisco: Jossey-Bass, 2009.

———. *Let Your Life Speak*. San Francisco: Jossey-Bass, 1999.

Powers, Jessica. *The Selected Poetry of Jessica Powers*. Washington, DC: ICS Publications, 1999.

Rilke, Rainer Maria. *Letters to a Young Poet*. New York: W. W. Norton & Company, 1993.

Singh, Kathleen Dowling. *The Grace in Aging*. New York: HarperSanFrancisco, 1998.

Tagore, Rabindranath. *The Gitanjali*. New York: Macmillan, 1971.

Taylor, Barbara Brown. "This Place That Has Made Us Kin: An Interview with Barbara Brown Taylor." By Jordan Thrasher. *Flycatcher Journal,* http://floatingintheblue.blogspot.com/2012/04/barbara-brown-taylor-on-thin-places.html.

Teresa of Avila. *The Collected Works of St. Teresa of Avila*. Washington, DC: ICS Publications, 1971.

Thomsen, Sara. "Darkness Cover Me." *Fertile Ground*, compact disc.

Wiederkehr, Macrina. *Abide: Keeping Vigil with the Word of God*. Collegeville, MN: Liturgical Press, 2011.

Wilcox, Ella Wheeler. *The Heart of the New Thought*. n.p.: CreateSpace Publishing, 2016.

Williamson, Marianne. *A Return to Love*. New York: HarperCollins, 1996.

ALPHABETICAL LISTING OF PRAYERS

A

B

C

D

E

F

G

H

I

L

M

N

O

*J*oyce Rupp is well known for her work as a writer, international retreat leader, and conference speaker. She is the author of numerous bestselling books, including *Praying Our Goodbyes*, *Open the Door*, and *Fragments of Your Ancient Name*. *Fly While You Still Have Wings* is among her publications earning an award in the spirituality books category from the Catholic Press Association. Rupp is a member of the Servite (Servants of Mary) community and the codirector of the Institute of Compassionate Presence. She lives in West Des Moines, Iowa.